AF661784

BASIC ELEMENTS OF BANKING RULES AND REGULATIONS

BASIC ELEMENTS OF BANKING RULES AND REGULATIONS

Data Ram Joshi

CYBER TECH PUBLICATIONS
4264/3, Ansari Road, Daryaganj, New Delhi-110002 (India)
Ph.: 011-23244078, 011-43559448 Fax: 011-23280028
E-Mail: cyberpublicationsdelhi@yahoo.com
Website: www.cybertechpublications.com

BASIC ELEMENTS OF BANKING RULES AND REGULATIONS

Data Ram Joshi

© Reserved

First Edition 2010

All rights reserved. No part of this publication may be reproduced, stored in a retrieval system or transmitted, in any form or by any means, electronic, mechanical, photo copying, recording or otherwise, without the prior permission of the publisher.

Asian Offset Printer

Published by :

G.S. Rawat for **Cyber Tech Publications**
4264/3, Ansari Road, Daryaganj, New Delhi-110002 (India)
Ph.: 011-23244078, 011-43559448 Fax: 011-23280028
E-Mail: cyberpublicationsdelhi@yahoo.com
Website: www.cybertechpublications.com

Preface

This book attempts to demystify the word 'banking technology' and offers much broader meaning and more realistic and operationally sufficient perspective on 'banking technology'. Although 'banking' is an old activity and has its roots in economics, finance and commerce, the word 'banking technology' is of recent origin. To many people 'banking technology' means the use of computers and related hardware to streamline and automate banking operations.

Further, such banks are very sensitive to the risks they face in dealing with money in the form of credit risk, or market risk or operational risk. Banks continuously embrace, with great fervor, the latest developments in information and communication technologies and customer relationship management in order to service customers better and reap more profits.

This book brings together research contributions from several academics and industrial professionals in all the three aspects mentioned above and conveys the message that banking technology and management. If banks employ cutting edge technologies to service their customers effectively and efficiently, regulatory requirements such as Basel II also force the banks to implement these technologies to enable uniform banking services throughout the world.

—Author

CONTENTS

1

BASIC ELEMENTS OF BANKING

INTRODUCTION

The range of options for providing capital would facilitate banks with varying degrees of sophistication to adopt appropriate method with supervisory validation. RBI recognises that several of the concerns expressed and recommendations made by India and other emerging markets on the first consultative document have been taken into account and addressed in the second consultative document. In this context, the Basel Committee's concerns for the constraints which are faced by the emerging markets and greater outreach by involving non G-10 countries in the standards setting exercise would lead to greater appreciation. However, some of the issues in the context of emerging markets are still to be addressed. RBI feels that the complexity and sophistication of the proposals restricts its universal application in emerging markets, where the banks continue to be the major segment in financial intermediation and would be facing considerable challenges in adopting all the proposals.

The increasing reliance on external rating agencies in the regulatory process would undermine the initiatives of banks in enhancing their risk management policies and practices and internal control systems. The minimum standards set even for the Internal Rating Based (IRB) foundation approach are complex and beyond the reach of many banks.

The emerging markets with their low technical skills, structural rigidities and less robust legal system, etc. would face serious implementation challenges. RBI, therefore, feels that the spirit of flexibility, universal applicability and discretion to national supervisors, consistent with the macro economic conditions specific to emerging markets.

Kinds of Elements

- + **Borrowing** – Allows program administrators or covered entities to use allowances that will be issued in future years to meet current year compliance requirements. There is usually a requirement to "pay back" these allowances (perhaps with interest) by reducing emissions in excess of the required reductions (over-compliance) in the future.
- + **Banking** - Allows covered entities to save or "bank" any excess allowances for future use, or to sell later on. This can encourage early compliance and/or over compliance.
- + **Compliance Period** – A compliance period is the length of time that covered entities have to submit allowances equivalent to their emissions, or face a penalty. Lengthening the compliance period can provide flexibility to covered entities, especially as/if the cap is lowered over time.
- **Safety Valves** – A safety valve is a mechanism that triggers a change in some aspect of the cap and trade program, if the compliance costs are higher then expected. In most instances, the mechanism is a pre-determined allowance price ceiling (allowance price cap) that when exceeded will trigger additional cost containment measures. Such measures could include extending the compliance period, increasing the availability of offsets, expanding the use of borrowing, etc.

The structure of the safety valve has the potential to effect the ability of the cap and trade program achieving its emissions reduction goal. For example, if exceeding the allowance price ceiling triggers the release of additional allowances into the market, the overall emissions cap will be effectively be raised.

- **Linkages** – allowing interaction or linkage between cap and trade programs (national, regional) expands the market of available compliance options and leads to more opportunities for low-cost emissions reductions and new technologies. Structural elements of the interacting cap and trade programs need to be comparable in order to facilitate linkage.

Scope of Coverage: Identifies what type of emissions will be regulated under the cap and trade program.

- **Gases** - What types of greenhouse gases will be regulated. All 6 major types, only CO2, or some combination?
- **Sectors** - What economic sectors will be regulated? Economy-wide, electric power production only, or some combination?

Point of Regulation: Identifies what entities will be required to hold allowances equivalent to their emissions.

- Upstream (suppliers of fossil fuels) – would require importers or suppliers of fossil fuels to submit allowances to cover the carbon in the products they sell.
- Downstream (direct emitter of GHGs) – this is a source-based system where direct emitters of GHGs are required to submit allowances to cover their emissions.
- Product-Based (Load-Based) – entities that are responsible for emissions associate with the production of electricity, natural gas, or other products provided to customers would be required to submit allowances to cover associated emissions. This would be a combination of both upstream and downstream regulation.
- Cap on Emissions (GHG Reduction Target) – The cap is the sum of all allowed emissions from all included facilities. The cap is often decreased over time.
- Timeline to Achieve Goal – How fast reductions will be required. This corresponds to the incremental reduction of the cap.

ALLOCATION OF ALLOWANCES

Allowances are a tradable commodity that basically affords the covered entity the 'right to emit'. One allowance is typically equal to one ton of carbon dioxide equivalent (CO_2e). Total amount of allowances is equivalent to the overall emissions cap. At the end of each compliance period, entities identified under the scope and point of regulation of the legislation (i.e. "covered entities") are responsible for submitting allowances equivalent to the level of their emissions.

The method of distributing allowances will affect the overall cost of the program and the distribution of those costs. There are three approaches to distributing allowances:

- **Free Allocation:** Free allocation can be fixed or updated. Updating allows for changes in the allocation of allowances overtime as levels of input, outputs or emissions change. This may affect future behavior of covered entities, sometimes in unintended ways.
  - *Grandfathering* – Free allocation based on covered entities' historic emissions. Must give credit for early action.
  - *Output-Based* – Free allocation based on the output of a product in a given sector (for example, allowances distributed by megawatt hour generated, or by tons of product manufactured). Can also be based on inputs.
- **Auction** – Allowances can be auctioned and the revenue generated can be used by the government to provide relief for compliance or high energy costs, fund complimentary policies, promote technology deployment, etc. The impact on covered entities will depend on the competitiveness within their respective industry, regulatory environment, and ability to pass on compliance costs to customers.
- **Combination** – A combination of free allocation and auctioning can be utilized to combine the benefits of both approaches. Auctioning can also be phased-in, after

an initial period of free allocation.

Cost Control Mechanisms: Several cost containment strategies are available to help manage the cost of compliance for covered entities.

- **Offsets** – covered entities may purchase verified emission reduction offsets generated through emission reduction projects undertaken outside of the cap and trade program. Offsets add flexibility and lower the overall cost of the program by bringing in low-cost emission reduction opportunities from outside of the cap.
- **Temporal Flexibility** – Inter-temporal trading provides additional flexibility to achieve compliance.

OTHER CONSIDERATIONS

Credit for Early Action – How to provide credit to those covered entities that chose to reduce their emissions in advance of any requirement to do so must be determined.

BASIC ELEMENTS OF THE CAPITALISM

It is possible to discern a gradual shift of emphasis in our classic theorists' analyses of the capitalist economy. Each gives special – but not exclusive – attention to a particular element. Although Smith devoted considerable attention to the way in which capital 'stock' was used to employ labour, he focused on the rapid extension of the division of labour and market exchange in eighteenth-century 'commercial' society. By Marx's time in the mid-nineteenth century, the enterprise factory system was more firmly established, the struggles between capital and labour had intensified, and cycles of economic expansion and contraction had increased in severity and frequency. By the end of the century, more attention was given to the expanding banking system and the increasing role of capital markets. But Schumpeter realized that money, banking and finance had been capitalism's most distinctive characteristics from the very earliest stages of development and that these were the key to understanding the system's operation. Obviously, Smith and

Marx were not unaware of the monetary and financial side of capitalism, but they looked elsewhere for its definitive features. With Keynes, as we have seen, money takes on even more significance.

Taking these accounts as a whole we can identify three fundamental elements, or institutional clusters, of the capitalist economy:

(a) monetary system for producing bank-credit money;

(b) market exchange; and

(c) private enterprise production of commodities.

(a) MONETARY SYSTEM AND BANK-CREDIT MONEY

Market exchange and enterprise production cannot exist without a viable monetary system. First, the impersonal coordination of sellers and buyers – that is, supply and demand– by price signals in large-scale markets presupposes theexistence of a means of exchange and payment. Second, as Weber emphasized, the calculation of costs of production and net profits in the enterprise requires a monetary standard of value (money of account). Third, money-capital for both production and financial speculation is created with loans (debt), produced by a network of banking enterprises which realize a profit from interest. Following Schumpeter, it could be argued that the financing of production with money- capital in the form newly created bank money uniquely specifies capitalism as a form of economic system. Enterprises, wage labour and market exchange existed to some small degree, at least, in many previous economic systems, but, as we shall see, their expansion into the dominant mode of production was made possible by the entirely novel institution of a money-producing banking system. Capital is 'that sum of means of payment which is available at any moment for transference to entrepreneurs'.

(b) MARKET EXCHANGE

The exchange of commodities in markets is based on competition between buyers (demand) and sellers (supply), which produces a price at which exchange is acceptable. This mechanism of bids (demand) and offers (supply) coordinates the three phases in the capitalist production of commodities:

(i) finance (money-capital) ?

(ii) production (capital + labour)?

(iii) consumption.

Bank credit finances investment (in the form of loans, stocks and shares) in physical capital and the employment of labour for the production of both the means of production and of consumption goods in order to realize a profit.

As we shall see, capitalism also contains purely speculative markets in financial assets which involve purely exchanges.

All forms of property, goods and services, including the enterprise and its potential revenue, are marketable as financial assets – stocks and shares, bonds, securities and so on. The uncertainty of financial asset price changes over time gives rise to speculative markets involving purely financial exchange in which assets are bought and sold in the expectation of price changes deals.

In this way, capital is endowed with a dual character – as both productive resource and speculative financial asset. Thus capitalism contains the following basic markets:

a. the money and money-capital markets by which the supply and demand for finance is coordinated and its price (interest) established;

b. the labour market which determines wages;

c. two markets involved in production:

    (i) the market for production goods (means of production); and

    (ii) the final consumption goods; and

d. financial asset markets, based on the fact that the title to the ownership of all forms of property in capitalism is represented as a marketable 'asset'.

As the discussion of our theorists has shown, there are two quite divergent analyses of these interrelations. On the one hand, theories deriving from Smith's account of the 'invisible hand' emphasize the effectiveness of the market's decen tralizedcoordination and integration of complex economic systems.

In this model of capitalism, competition produces the most efficient outcome in which all resources are fully utilized. Moreover, economic agents – bankers, workers, managers and so on – are rewarded in accord with their functional contribution, which is, in turn, determined by a competitive process of supply and demand. For example, a shortage in the supply of highly productive labour will lead to the substitution of labour-saving physical capital. Furthermore, this approach strongly implies that the economic integration and efficiency creates social integration by binding economic agents together in webs of mutually beneficial exchange. On the other hand, Marx, Weber and – to some extent – Keynes point to the power inequalities of the property rights between economic classes and agents and to the fact that the divided economic functions do not simply cooperate, but struggle over the surplus. For example, capital, but not wage- labour, has the right to control the operation of the enterprise and to calculate and distribute profits. Furthermore, this tradition places emphasis on the unintended negative or contradictory effects of market coordination.

By enabling capital to be withdrawn from unprofitable activity and reinvested elsewhere, financial asset markets are an essential source of capitalism's flexibility and dynamism. But, as Keynes warned, this capacity can quickly incapacitate the economy if there is a widespread withdrawal of capital from production and/or consumption and its storage of capital in the form of money. Furthermore, pure speculation under conditions of uncertainty can routinely create asset price bubbles and instability that can perturb the production of goods and services.

Despite these different views on the efficacy and stability of the market mechanism, there is widespread agreement that market competition accelerates economic growth by driving capitalist entrepreneurs constantly to revolutionize the means of production in a process described by Schumpeter as 'creative destruction'.

(c) PRIVATE ENTERPRISE PRODUCTION OF COMMODITIES

The production of goods and services for sale on the market takes place in private enterprises which are institutionally separated from the household and state, where consumption takes place. Money-capital and wage labour are brought together in the enterprise, which aims to calculate the net cost of producing marketable commodities with an exchange value in order to realize a monetary profit. All means of production are the private property of the enterprise and constitute its physical or material capital. Production is undertaken by legally free labour, employed for wages by the enterprise.

The physical means and money used in the process of production are 'capital' in that they are not owned or controlled by those who directly operate the enterprise – workers and managers. In other words, as Marx explains, capital is not defined by its functional role in the process of production, but by a power relation. 'Money' becomes money 'capital' only with the existence of property-less labour – that is to say, a class of economic agents that can only subsist by selling their only 'property' – their labour power.

With the development of the large-scale corporation, comprising shareholders and salaried managers, it was widely held that private ownership had been separated from control of the enterprise to such an extent that capitalism was no longer an accurate designation of modern economies. However, as we shall see in chapter 6, both ownership and control of capital remain highly concentrated and outside the control of almost all employees.

Private ownership is not necessary for the physical means of production to be capital. States also own means of production, but if workers do not exercise control over their deployment, use and disposal, then it is more appropriate to refer to this as a form of 'state capitalism', rather than socialism.

From this standpoint, for example, Saudi Arabia's oil and gas enterprise Saudi Aramco and Mexico's Pemex, as well as communist China's enterprises, are state capitalist. Again, the enterprise – like the market – can be looked at from two perspectives – as the functionally efficient means for the coordination of economic activity, or as the source of exploitation and site of the most intense conflict between economic agents and classes. These different conceptions of the enterprise will be examined in chapter 6, but here we should note that coordination within the enterprise is not based on the 'invisible hand'. As Marx and Weber insisted, the wage contract does not merely specify the terms of the contractual exchange of effort for reward; it also entails the workers' subordination to the 'visible' authority of the owners and controllers of capital.

These elements A, B, and C comprise a structurally differentiated 'economy' which is, in Polanyi's terms, 'dis-embedded' from other non-economic institutions in society.Decisions about production and distribution of goods and services in the market capitalist economy are taken on the basis of an economic rationality – that is, costs of production and relative prices. In pre-market society the organization of production and distribution is 'embedded' in families, communities, manorial households or states. For example, the division of labour in simple hunter-gatherer societies was embedded in communal and familial relations. Men made tools and weapons and hunted; women made utensils, gathered vegetation and cooked. All labour was devoted to production for basic subsistence and use, not exchange; and distribution was governed by norms of in-group reciprocity.

Traditional agrarian communities largely distributed production in accordance with an ethic or charity. In empires – such as ancient Egypt – the surplus was collected and redistributed as rations by the central bureaucracy. However, as we shall see, two crucially important related points must be borne in mind. First, the separation of the economy as a complex of distinct institutions does not mean that it is completely separate and autonomous from the other parts of society. Second, the market and other basic elements of the capitalist economy are not self-reproducing or self- regulating – that is to say, Smith's 'perfect liberty' of freely contracted exchange relations did not emerge spontaneously. Rather, the 'free' market and all other institutions of the capitalist system – the enterprise, the banking system and so on – are all produced and maintained by state law, norms and cultural beliefs. As Marx emphasized in his critique of Smith, the revenues (rent, profits/interest and wages) received by the factors of production (land, capital and labour) were the result of the social relations of production – that is, property relations. Property gives capital the legal right to organize production in the enterprise. These issues will be examined further in part II; here we need simply to outline the main points for consideration.

In simple terms and notwithstanding considerable variations between different countries and across time, relationships between the state and the structurally distinct market capitalist economy are the outcome of the mutual accommodation between the emerging capitalist bourgeoisie and the early modern state, described by Weber as the 'memorable alliance'. The struggle between monarchs and merchants for control of opportunities for profit-making was resolved by a tacit agreement in which the bourgeoisie ceded their claim to rule in exchange for the right to make money in conditions secured and protected by the state. In return, the state was financed by taxation and loans from the propertied classes. In short, as we shall see in more detail in part II, capitalism is characterized by two interdependent sources of power – the state's legitimate use of force and the private ownership and control of economic resources (capital). Modern capitalist states provide:

(i) a level of social order within which peaceful economic activity can take place;

(ii) an institutional and legal framework which specifies the rights of the various economic agents and the rules of competition and exchange – that is, the laws governing property rights and contracts between buyers and sellers;

(iii) a range of services and 'public goods' that would appear to be necessary for an effective capitalist economy, but which private enterprise is either reluctant or unable to undertake – for example, a sound currency, education and welfare to maintain the quality of the work force ('human capital'); and

(iv) attempts to correct the market's failure to achieve acceptable outcomes – for example, financial crises or persistent unemployment. In return, these activities are financed by taxation and loans with the consent of the economic interests of civil society. Each of these 'functions' can be considered from the different perspectives on the operation of the capitalist system that we have encountered. Some would argue that the state's actions are based upon a disinterested search for the most effective and efficient means of running capitalism. Others contend that the regulation of the economy is the outcome of a conflict between irreconcilable interests that does not necessarily produce the most efficient outcome. In this regard, the Marxist perspective maintains that the state exists to ensure the dominance of capital and subordination of labour.

The scale and scope of the state's direct intervention and participation in the economy is continuously contested in a way that could almost be said to define the nature of politics in modern capitalist societies. On the one hand economic liberals, taking Smith as their guide, argue that the market has a capacity for self-regulation and, consequently, state involvement should be kept to a minimum.

On the other hand, radical critiques, based in varying degrees on Marx, contend that market capitalism is crisis-prone and founded on economic inequality. State power should be used to curtail the depredations and destructive consequences of the capitalist class. Various 'middle' or 'third' ways have been sought, which seek to harness the productive efficiency of market capitalism to the attainment of politically determined goals and values – equality of opportunity, social justice, the eradication of poverty, health and even 'happiness' (for a critical survey of 'third way' discourse. The balance of power and interdependence between states and capital is characterized by a particular articulation of sovereign territorial space and market networks at the international level. Although capitalism is dependent on the social peace that states can bring about, it is by nature extra-territorial. In the most fundamental terms, what we now see as globalization may be understood as an acceleration of the process whereby capitalist networks and markets extend across the world. In this process, the complex relationship between the two 'logics' of political and economic power is revealed.

As we shall see, the idea that there exists a mutually reinforcing connection, or 'elective affinity', between the liberal democratic state and capitalism is well established in the social and historical sciences. Most obviously, as we have noted, Smith's 'perfect liberty' of the market has its foundation in the politically liberal state.

Weber agreed and drew further connections between citizenship and capitalism. Furthermore, it is argued that modern representative democracy is an almost inevitable consequence of economic and political liberty. As I have already suggested, these issues are of the utmost contemporary importance as capitalism continues to spread across the world and in doing so encounters hitherto unreceptive regimes and forms of state in Islamic countries and communist China.

MONEY CENTER BANKS

The experience of most people with banks is at the retail level -- making deposits, writing checks, and perhaps taking consumer loans or small business loans. These activities, while important to individuals, represent a minor part of the banking business. For an understanding of the major role that banks play in the economy, we need to look at the activities of truly large banks.

What is a Money Center Bank?

The U.S. is unique among the nations in terms of the number of commercial banks in operation, 7,660 as of September

2004. This number has been steadily decreasing due to mergers, but is still about five times greater than that in the U.K., the nation with the second largest number of banks. Most of the assets of U.S. banks are concentrated in the larger banks. The ten largest now hold almost half the total of bank assets.

The nation's largest banks are often referred to as money market banks or money center banks. In addition to the traditional markets, to be a money center bank today means to have a global presence as well as heavy involvement in wholesale banking with clients comprising many retail banks and large corporations. Citibank, J P Morgan Chase, and Bank of America fit this description.

What Do They Do?

The activities of money market banks may be classified into four businesses: portfolio business, corporate finance, trading, and distribution. Each of these will be described briefly.

Portfolio business is the activity of asset accumulation and funding in the interest of what is best for the bank. The bank acquires assets, securities or loans, which it can fund at a spread over its cost of money. It seeks to enhance that spread by mismatching its maturities when rates and its view of rates indicate that it is likely to be profitable.

Corporate finance is the business related to old-style lending, and is focused on what is best for the client, with the bank's reward a fee for service. The bank explores opportunities for the client: a loan or a public offering like commercial paper, and assists the client in obtaining the required funds however they may be structured.

Trading is a traditional part of banking, but is now more for market making and liquidity than in the past. A strategy of money center banks today is to aggressively make loans with the notion that they will sell off to investors, at a slight markup, participations in those loans. This activity also helps support their corporate finance activity.

Distribution involves the sale of its own paper and exempt securities -- treasuries, agencies, general obligation munis, BAs,

Euro CDs, and other money market paper -- that banks are permitted to trade. Today those sales have been extended into participations in bank loans and commercial paper. A substantial sales force with special skills is required in this activity.

Bank Liquidity

Liquidity for a bank means the ability to meet its financial obligations as they come due. Bank lending finances investments in relatively illiquid assets, but it fund its loans with mostly short term liabilities. Thus one of the main challenges to a bank is ensuring its own liquidity under all reasonable conditions.

Asset Management Banking

Commercial banks differ widely in how they manage liquidity. A small bank derives its funds primarily from customer deposits, normally a fairly stable source in the aggregate. Its assets are mostly loans to small firms and households, and it usually has more deposits than it can find creditworthy borrowers for. Excess funds are typically invested in assets that will provide it with liquidity such as Fed funds loaned and U.S. government securities. The holding of assets that can readily be turned into cash when needed, is known as asset management banking.

THE FEDERAL RESERVE SYSTEM

This overview of the Federal Reserve System is a digest of the publication The Federal Reserve System, Purposes and Functions, 8th edition, December 1994, by the Federal Reserve Board of Governors. Financial panics plagued the nation throughout much of the 19th century. Many bank failures, business bankruptcies, and economic downturns could be traced to a poorly regulated banking system and the lack of a flexible money supply. A particularly severe crisis in 1907 finally led Congress to establish the National Monetary Commission to propose an institution that could deal with those problems.

After considerable debate, Congress passed the Federal Reserve Act which Woodrow Wilson signed into law on Dec 23, 1913. The act stated that its purposes were to "provide for the establishment of Federal reserve banks, to furnish an elastic currency, to afford means of rediscounting commercial paper, to establish a more effective supervision of banking in the United States, and for other purposes."

Over the years, deficiencies in the original act have been addressed in further legislation. The International Banking Act of 1978, sometimes known as the Humphrey-Hawkins Act, included an update of the objectives of the Federal Reserve, namely to achieve economic growth in line with the economy's potential to expand; a high level of employment; stable prices (meaning stability in the purchasing power of the dollar); and moderate long-term interest rates.

Basic Duties

The Federal Reserve comprises the Board of Governors in Washington D.C., and twelve regional Federal Reserve Banks. Their responsibilities are to:

- Conduct the nation's monetary policy by influencing the money and credit conditions in the economy.
- Supervise and regulate banking institutions to ensure safety and soundness of the nation's banking and financial system.
- Maintain the stability of the financial system.
- Provide certain financial services to the U.S. government, financial institutions, the public, and foreign official institutions, including a major role in operating the nation's payments system.

Board of Governors

The Board of Governors was established as a federal agency. It is made up of seven members appointed by the President and confirmed by the Senate. The full term of a member is fourteen years with appointments staggered so that one term expires on January 31 of each even-numbered year.

The Chairman of the Board is appointed for a four year term starting midway through each Presidential term. Besides carefully monitoring domestic and international financial and economic developments, the Board supervises and regulates the operations of the Federal Reserve Banks. The Board is supported by a Washington staff of about 1700.

The Board is audited annually by a major public accounting firm and is also subject to audit by the General Accounting Office, an arm of Congress. Monetary policy, which is exempt from audit by the GAO, is monitored directly by Congress through written reports prepared by the Board.

GETTING STARTED

Let's assume you raise $6 million in cash with help from other investors. That will be the bank's initial equity, the owner's stake. Next you obtain a charter, rent a building, furnish it with all the necessary equipment, hire and train a staff, and open your doors for business.

You'll need to deposit some of your initial stake at the Fed. Those funds will be used to clear checks written by your own depositors. You'll also need to keep enough cash in the vault to meet the demand for withdrawals by your depositors. Let's assume initial expenses of $1.2 million. That leaves $4.8 million, of which you allocate $2 million to vault cash and $2.8 million to your Fed account.

Managing Loans and Other Investments

As your business develops, some customers will deposit their own money to open checking accounts. Others will invest in your savings accounts and certificates of deposit (term loans) which must pay a competitive interest rate. Still others will seek loans from the bank. It is up to you to determine whether prospective borrowers are good credit risks, and will be able to pay the interest charges and return the principal on the specified date.

Accounting Needs

In managing your bank, you will need an accounting system to determine how your decisions are likely to affect the bank's profitability. The most important account is the balance sheet. This shows at any given moment, the bank's assets (what it owns), its liabilities (what it owes to others), and its net worth (what belongs to the owners). Net worth, or equity, is equal to assets minus liabilities. Your equity should remain positive and preferably growing. If it ever gets too low relative to total assets, your regulator may close the bank.

Balance Sheet and Earnings Forecasts

If your bank does well, the balance sheet will expand with new assets and liabilities. The equity should also increase, assuming you retain some of the profits in the bank rather than pay them all out as dividends to the owners. You started with initial equity of $6 million. Let's take a look at the balance sheet after you have been in business for some time. It is shown together with an earnings forecast for the coming year.

The earnings forecast is based on expected earning rates of the bank's assets and the cost of borrowed funds. Also shown is the expected cost of operations or fixed costs, covering rent, insurance, utilities, salaries, etc. The entries in blue are items that you might try to modify to see how they would affect the key performance measure, the return on equity. Of course, you must maintain the required minimum ratios set by the regulators.

Growth Management

Note that your equity has grown from $6.0 million to $10.5 million due to retained earnings. You have acquired a substantial amount in deposits, some of which are ordinary checking accounts that pay no interest. Others were borrowed at market rates. All deposits whether or not they bear interest have associated costs.

With the additional funds available from deposits, you have redistributed your assets to what you hope will enhance future earnings: $5.0 million in reserves, $7.7 million in T-bills, $1.1 million in loans to other banks, and $110 million in ordinary loans. You project net earnings for the coming year after taxes of $1.51 million. That would be a return on equity of 14.38%

and a return on assets of 1.21%, which is quite reasonable performance.

Required Operating Ratios

In the lower left corner of the table are the three ratios that must be kept above minimum values established by bank regulators. The capital ratio is the ratio of a bank's equity to a risk-weighted sum of the bank's assets. The weightings are 0 for reserves, 0 for government securities, 0.2 for loans to banks, and 1.0 for ordinary loans. A minimum capital ratio of 8% is required.

The leverage ratio is the ratio of a bank's equity to the unweighted sum of its total assets. The required minimum is 3%. The reserve ratio is the ratio of a bank's reserves (deposits at the Fed plus vault cash) to its demand deposits, i.e. checking deposits. The required minimum is 10% for large banks, but only 3% on the first $45.4 million of demand deposits, which is the case for your small bank.

How Transactions Affect Operating Ratios

When a bank issues an ordinary loan, its assets (A) and liabilities (L) increase equally. Its reserves (R) remain unchanged, which results in a decrease in its reserve ratio (R/L). Its equity, i.e. capital (C = A-L) remains unchanged, which results in a decrease in its capital ratio (C/A).

When the borrower spends the funds, assuming they end up in a different bank, R, A, and L decrease equally. Since R is normally a small fraction of L, the reserve ratio decreases by an amount roughly equal to the fractional change in R. Since C is normally a small fraction of A, the capital ratio increases by an amount roughly equal to the fractional change in A.

When the borrower pays interest on the loan out of a deposit within the bank, L decreases while A and R remain unchanged. This results in an increase in both the reserve ratio and the capital ratio. If the borrower pays interest from an outside source, A and R increase while L remains unchanged. This results in an increase in both the reserve ratio and the capital ratio.

When the borrower repays the loan from a deposit within the bank, R remains unchanged while A and L decrease equally. This results in an increase in both the reserve ratio and the capital ratio. If the borrower repays the loan from an outside source, R increases while A and L remain unchanged. This results in an increase in reserve ratio but no change in the capital ratio.

When a bank buys something for itself, it may issue a bank draft in payment. If the recipient deposits the draft in the same bank, he receives a deposit which increases L, while A and R remain unchanged. If he deposits it in another bank, A and R decrease while L remains unchanged. In both cases, the capital ratio and reserve ratio of the issuing bank decrease..

Liability Management Banking

In contrast, large banks generally lack sufficient deposits to fund their main business -- dealing with large companies, governments, other financial institutions, and wealthy individuals. Most borrow the funds they need from other major lenders in the form of short term liabilities which must be continually rolled over. This is known as liability management, a much riskier method than asset management. A small bank will lose potential income if gets its asset management wrong. A large bank that gets its liability management wrong may fail.

Key to Liability Management

The key to liability management is always being able to borrow. Therefore a bank's most vital asset is its creditworthiness. If there is any doubt about its credit, lenders can easily switch to another bank. The rate a bank must pay to borrow will go up rapidly with the slightest suspicion of trouble. If there is serious doubt, it will be unable to borrow at any rate, and will go under.

In recent years, large banks have been making increasing use of asset management in order to enhance liquidity, holding a larger part of their assets as securities as well as securitizing their loans to recycle borrowed funds.

Bank Runs

A bank run is an overwhelming demand for cash by a bank's depositors. With the advent of deposit insurance, bank runs by small depositors are largely a thing of the past. Insurance is limited to $100,000 per deposit, which provides complete coverage to about 99% of all depositors. But it covers only about three-fourths of the total amount of deposits because many accounts far exceed the insurance limits.

A large depositor assumes a risk and needs to know something about the bank's own balance sheet. However a healthy balance sheet does not eliminate all risk. Even if the depositor knows the bank has adequate liquidity, others may not. Large depositors must therefore be concerned about what others are likely to believe. A rumor about a bank, even though unfounded, can trigger a run that causes a solvent bank to fail.

Possible Solutions

The problems with deposit insurance could be solved by restricting its coverage to risk-free narrow banks or narrow deposits. A narrow bank would offer checking deposits and would be allowed to invest only in safe liquid assets such as T-bills. It could operate as a separate institution or as a subsidiary of a bank holding company. Only narrow banks would be eligible for deposit insurance.

Narrow deposits would be checking deposits that could be offered by any licensed institution on condition that they were secured exclusively by safe liquid assets. Only narrow deposits would be eligible for deposit insurance. Thus narrow banks or narrow deposits would be fully collateralized, and deposit insurance would be redundant and unnecessary. Ending deposit insurance would greatly reduce the moral hazard problem in banking.

A Fully-Backed Depository System

Banks in a Fully-Backed System

In a fully-backed system, every bank would have to hold reserves equal to the full value of its demand deposits. Reserves are held on deposit at the Fed and as vault cash. We will call the deposit at the Fed its reserve account. For its investment activities the bank would need additional funds at the Fed, which we will call its investment account. When the bank spends, the Fed would debit the bank's investment account and credit the reserve account of the payee's bank, while the payee receives a new credit in his own bank account.

Banks could create deposits through lending, but credit money would cease to exist. A bank could no longer simply credit a deposit to fund a loan, as in a fractional reserve system. It would have to transfer funds from its investment account to its reserve account to cover the new deposit. That would increase the M1 money aggregate, defined as the total of demand deposits plus cash in circulation, but it would have no effect on the monetary base.

Banks must hold enough cash to meet the withdrawal demands of their depositors. To acquire cash, banks would draw on their reserve accounts. That simply swaps one form of reserves for another without changing the total. Cash withdrawals or deposits by bank customers have no effect on the M1 money aggregate.

The Fed as the Sole Depository

In a fully-backed system, there are good reasons for transferring the depository role of banks to the Fed. The depository and payment functions of a bank are basically clerical, and offer little opportunity for income other than fees for service. Banks would have less incentive to seek new demand deposits since the reserves backing them could not be used to support new lending.

With a single depository, all deposits would exist as entries in a common computer system. Verifying balances and making payments could be done instantly, thereby eliminating checking system float with its logistic cost and complexities. The two-tier system of base money and bank money would be replaced by a one-tier system of base money alone, all created by the Fed. The entire money supply would consist of deposits at the

Fed and circulating cash. That means the Fed would have total control of the money supply.

All deposits would be transaction deposits. The Fed would not offer interest-earning term deposits since they would be redundant with government securities which are the functional equivalent of term deposits. Deposit insurance would not be needed or appropriate. It is worth noting that when private banks no longer serve as depositories, the concept of bank reserves loses its meaning.

Henceforth, we will assume that the Fed is the sole depository, operating through local branches which we will call banks. Any economic entity, whether a financial firm, a non-financial firm, or an individual, would be eligible to open a transaction account at a branch bank. Former banks would lose their depository role and become non-bank financial intermediaries, which we will refer to as Financial Service Companies (FSCs). They could sell their branches to the Fed and/or merge with existing intermediaries. FSCs already create most of the loans on which the economy runs. In this system, they would create essentially all of them.

Monetary Policy Options

The basic goal of monetary policy is to provide financial liquidity as needed to support a growing economy while limiting the inflation rate to some small value, typically about 2 percent per year. Monetary policy can be implemented in two ways: (1) control of the money supply growth rate, which leaves the money market interest rate as a residual, or (2) control of the money market interest rate, which leaves the money supply as a residual. The money market rate is the interest rate at which major FSCs lend money to each other on a short-term basis, say 30 days. It is analogous to the London Inter-Bank Offer Rate (LIBOR) on 30-day Eurodollar placements.

Some economists have advocated option (1) with a fixed growth rate of the base money supply consistent with the potential growth rate of the real economy plus a small inflation rate. A key objection to this is its inflexibility. There are certain to be significant external shocks to the economy from time to time. The negative impact of such shocks could be lessened with adjustments in interest rates, which a fixed money growth rate policy would not allow. Furthermore the potential growth rate exhibits long term variations for a number of reasons, which makes determination of an optimum fixed rate problematic.

Option (2) is adopted here because it provides the flexibility to deal with unexpected conditions. It is also more effective in limiting interest rate volatility. Firms cannot plan efficiently if interest rates vary sharply and unpredictably. Selecting the optimal interest rate at any given time is not easy, and mistakes have been made. However a great deal of experience now exists in many different economies which support the overall effectiveness of the interest rate targeting option.

Monetary Policy Implementation

The Fed steers the money market interest rate toward the target rate through its open market operations. When the interest rate rises above the target rate, the Fed purchases securities in the open market to increase the aggregate supply of deposits. When the interest rate falls below the target rate, the Fed sells securities. In this way it continually adjusts the supply of loanable funds to meet the demand at approximately the target rate.

In the fractional reserve system, the Fed controls the money market interest rate by operating directly on the reserves of banks. Since the loanable funds supply is a much larger pool of money, interest rate control in a fully-backed system will be less responsive to the Fed's open market operations, and will therefore require far more funds.

The normal growth bias of the economy creates the need for an expanding money supply. In order to maintain control of the overnight lending rate, on average the Fed must purchase securities from the public to support the demand. That means the Fed's portfolio of securities will continue to grow with time.

Financial Capital Formation

FSCs perform a vital role in the economy. They pool the savings of investors and make them available to borrowers. They sell financial instruments as diverse as debt securities, mutual funds, and insurance policies. In issuing loans they increase the amount of private sector debt. In principle there is no limit to how large private debt can grow. In practice private debt should not exceed what borrowers can safely cover with their existing wealth or with their own income as payments become due.

Even though the amount of debt increases as a function of demand, the money supply remains unchanged until the Fed acts to change it. However the Fed has to provide whatever new money is needed to hold the interest rate in line with its target rate, as long as its monetary policy is based on the interest-rate priority option. In the current fractional reserve system, most of the private sector debt is generated by FSCs rather than banks. In a fully-backed system, virtually all of the private sector debt would be generated by FSCs.

Dealing with Liquidity Problems of FSCs

An FSC in good standing may unconditionally borrow from the Fed, just as banks do now. The interest rate is set 100 basis points above money market target rate. This large spread means that FSCs will use the lending facility mainly to cover short term cash flow problems, and not as a source of funds to invest.

The loan must be collateralized by the borrower with Treasury securities. It may be rolled over indefinitely as long as the borrower has sufficient funds on deposit to pay the interest and to cover any change in the market value of the collateral.

FSCs eligible to borrow from the Fed should be limited to those in the "too large to fail" class. Other FSCs and non-financial firms with good credit should be able to borrow in the money market, just as households with good credit should be able to borrow from a FSC offering retail loans.

The Fed–Treasury Relationship

The Treasury sells securities to the Fed only to roll over the maturing securities in the Fed's portfolio. Otherwise all new Treasury securities are sold to the public. This ensures that the yields reflect the open market rate. The principal source of income for the Fed is the interest it earns on its Treasury securities. Periodically, the Fed remits any income in excess of its operating costs to the Treasury.

In a fractional reserve system, the Treasury holds most of its funds in commercial banks in order to facilitate the Fed's control of the Fed funds rate. In a fully-backed system with only Fed branch banks as depositories, the Treasury would hold all of its funds at the Fed. It must manage its cash flow to maintain its Fed account at a fixed level on average in order to minimize variations in the private sector money supply. That means the Treasury must cover its deficit spending in a timely manner with the sale of its securities.

Minimizing the Risk of Systemic Failure

Cash flow is a constant concern for financial institutions. FSCs borrow to lend at a profit, but they differ widely in the degree to which they mismatch the maturity of their assets and liabilities. Mismatching creates a potential cash flow problem. Most FSCs borrow short and lend long, expecting to roll over their short term liabilities on a continuing basis. If their credit became suspect for any reason, they might be unable to refinance at all. There is nothing about a fully-backed system that would eliminate excessive risk taking by FSCs.

The risk of systemic failure arises from the cascading of liabilities of one FSC on another. A default by a major borrower could cause defaults by earlier lenders. To minimize this danger, capital adequacy requirements should be imposed on all FSCs considered "too large to fail". The required ratio of capital to risk-adjusted assets should be an increasing function of the mismatch in their maturities. This is similar to the capital adequacy requirements now imposed on banks, based on the Basel accord. The details of the formula need to be worked out, and will require careful study to ensure its effectiveness and practicability.

In a fully-backed system there is no need for deposit insurance. All deposits represent base money on deposit at the Fed. Government insurance should not be provided on the financial instruments offered by the FSCs. Bond rating agencies can expand their domain to rate the creditworthiness of FSCs as institutions. That would be of great value to investors, but more importantly it means that FSCs would tend to avoid practices that reflected badly on their creditworthiness in the competitive business of lending for a profit.

Advantages of a Fully-Backed System

There should be less temptation for FSCs to advance loans for purely speculative games. However the risk of too rapid growth through borrowing and lending would remain so capital adequacy rules should be extended to major FSCs as they are now to banks.

- It should be more robust than the fractional reserve system.
- It eliminates the need for deposit insurance and the moral hazard that can foster.
- With the Fed operating as the sole depository, payments can be cleared without delay, eliminating the nuisance of checking system float, and significantly reduce associated costs.
- It should end sterile games that banks play to get around the fractional reserve requirement, such as overnight sweep accounts..

Estimating the Base Money Supply

Since money earns no interest, firms and households will hold the minimum required to meet their liquidity needs. Holding money in excess of near-term needs represents a loss in purchasing power equal to the inflation rate, which has averaged about 3 percent over the long term. Alternatively, it represents an opportunity cost which varies with the money market interest rate.

If the fully-backed system were working in the U.S. today (2007), a rough estimate of the base money supply would include the currency in circulation ($750 billion), total demand deposits and other checkable deposits ($620 billion), overnight sweep accounts ($750 billion), and what FSCs would need for liquidity ($380 billion). The latter figure assumes liquidity equal to about 4% of total current assets of the banking system.

The estimated total base money supply would therefore be about $2,500 billion. That is an increase of about $1,750 billion from the current amount, which means the Fed would have to monetize that much of the $4,500 billion in Treasury securities held by the public.

Transition to a Fully-Backed System

The transition would not be easy. It would have to be carefully planned and phased in slowly enough to give all parties adequate time to make the necessary adjustments. Banks and thrifts would have to close out their existing loans, since they represent bank money that is no longer allowed under a fully-backed system. Some banks would probably sell out to existing FSCs. In some cases, existing bank loans would probably be sold to other FSCs as investments. Those remaining in business would have to close down their depository operations. Without the depository role, banks would no longer need the same number of branch offices. The Fed would probably offer to buy them in setting up its own depository branch offices. A logical way to proceed would be to gradually increase the reserve ratio requirement on existing depositories until it reached 100 percent.

Monetary Policy

The Federal Reserve conducts monetary policy using three major tools:

(1) open market operations to control the level of reserves in the depository system.

(2) setting reserve requirements for depository institutions, and

(3) setting the discount rate for lending reserves.

Policy regarding open market operations is the responsibility of the Federal Open Market Committee (FOMC) comprising the seven members of the Board, the president of the New York Federal Reserve Bank, and the presidents of four other reserve banks on a rotating basis. However, the Board has sole authority over changes in reserve requirements and the discount rate.

Federal Reserve Banks

Each Reserve Bank has its own board of nine directors chosen from outside the Bank. Three, designated Class A, represent commercial banks that are members of the Federal Reserve System. Three Class B and three Class C represent the public. The member commercial banks in each district elect the Class A and B directors. The Board of Governors appoints the Class C directors, one of whom it selects as chairman. No Class B or Class C director may be an officer, director, or employee of a bank or a bank holding company. The directors in turn nominate a president of the Reserve Bank, whose selection is subject to approval of the Board of Governors.

Reserve Bank Services

The twelve Federal Reserve Banks provide banking services to depository institutions within their district, and to the federal government. For depository institutions they maintain reserve and clearing accounts and provide various payment services. These include collecting checks, electronically transferring funds, and distributing and receiving currency and coin. For the federal government they act as fiscal agents. As such they maintain the Treasury Department's transaction account; pay Treasury checks; process electronic payments; and issue, transfer, and redeem U.S. government securities.

Income of the Federal Reserve

The income of the Federal Reserve System is derived primarily from the interest on U.S. government securities that it has acquired through open market operations. Other important sources of income are the interest on foreign currency investments held by the System, interest on loans to depository institutions, and fees for services provided to depository institutions such as check clearing, fund transfers, and automated clearing house operations.

After it pays its expenses, the Federal Reserve turns the rest of its earnings over to the U.S. Treasury. About 95% of net earnings have been paid into the Treasury since inception in 1914. The Board of Governors audits the Reserve Banks every year. The Reserve Banks, like the Board, are subject to audit by the GAO, but certain functions such as transactions with foreign central banks and open market operations are excluded from audit.

Member Banks

The nation's banks can be divided into three types according to which governmental body charters them and whether or not they are members of the Federal Reserve System. Those chartered by the federal government (through the Office of the Comptroller of the Currency in the Department of the Treasury) are national banks, and by law are members of the System.

Banks chartered by the states are divided into those that are members of the System and those that are not. State-chartered banks are not required to join the System, but they may elect to become members if they meet the standards. As of June 30, 2006, there were a total of 7,480 commercial banks nationwide, of which 2,548 were members of the System. The Federal Deposit Insurance Corporation is responsible for supervising non-member banks.

Member banks must subscribe to stock in their regional Federal Reserve Bank in an amount equal to 3 percent of their capital and surplus. They receive a 6 percent annual dividend on their stock and may vote for Class A and Class B directors of the Reserve Bank. However the stock does not carry with it the control and financial interest that is normal for the common stock of a for-profit organization. It offers no opportunity for capital gain and may not be sold or pledged as collateral for loans. The stock is merely a legal obligation that goes along with membership.

Independence of the Fed

The Federal Reserve System is considered to be an independent central bank. It is, but only in the sense that its decisions do not have to be ratified by the President or anyone else in the executive branch of government. However the entire system is subject to the oversight of Congress because the Constitution gives to Congress the power to coin money and set its value.

In 1913 Congress delegated that power to the Fed, and could reclaim it at any time. The Fed must act within the framework of the overall objectives of economic and financial policy established by Congress. Thus the description of the System as "independent within the government" is more accurate.

Fractional Reserve Banking

This article is a companion to Money Basics. It presents a more detailed treatment of fractional reserve banking and its relation to the money supply.

Reserve Requirements

All depository institutions -- commercial banks and thrifts -- in the United States are subject to reserve requirements on customer deposits. The required reserve ratio depends on the amount of checkable deposits a bank holds. No reserves are required on the first $9.3 million. Between $9.3 million and $43.9 million, deposits are subject to a 3% reserve. Above $43.9 million they are subject to a 10% reserve. These breakpoints were effective year-end 2007, and are adjusted annually in accordance with money supply growth. No reserves are required against time deposits or savings accounts.

Reserves are figured as the average held over a 14-day period, ending every second Wednesday. On any single day, a bank needs only enough to cover its customer's withdrawals.

A bank may hold its reserves in any combination of vault cash and deposits at the Fed. As profit-seeking enterprises, banks try to keep their reserves close to the required minimum, since they earn no interest.

How Banks Meet Reserve Requirements

A bank loses reserves whenever it pays out cash or transfers funds by wire for its customers. Customer checks to pay out of town bills funnel back through the Fed and are charged against its reserves. A bank may also lose reserves when it advances loans or buys securities. Conversely a bank gains reserves when it receives new deposits.

A bank facing a reserve deficiency has several options. It can try to borrow reserves for one or more days from another bank; sell marketable assets, such as government securities; bid for funds in the money market, such as large CDs or Eurodollars; or as a last resort it can pledge collateral and borrow at the Fed's discount window.

An active market in reserves acts to redistribute reserves to those banks that need them. However banks cannot create reserves themselves. If the aggregate demand exceeds the existing supply of non-borrowed reserves, the banking system as a whole has no alternative but to borrow more reserves from the Fed.

CULTURE AND CAPITALISM

Like all social systems, capitalism is 'cultural' in the sense that its economic activities are guided, framed and rendered meaningful to the participants by shared symbols, norms, beliefs and values. Attention has been given to two main issues: the 'spirit' of entrepreneurial capitalism, and acquisitive consumerism. Capitalism is historically distinctive in that both production and consumption are freed from the limits set by traditional cultural constraints. Some level of luxurious 'conspicuous consumption' is to be found in all except the simplest subsistence-level societies, but only in modern capitalism does it become a major motive force in the economy. In short, if the culture of capitalism is unable to generate an ever increasing expansion and proliferation of consumers' wants, then the economy falters and enters a period of stagnation.

As Weber observed in late nineteenth-century Silesia, where traditionally limited patterns of consumption had not entirely disappeared, it was proving futile to increase the peasants' output by offering monetary incentives. Raising the rates simply led the peasants to reduce their effort to the point that gave them the previous level to meet their customary level of consumption. Applying the same logic to enterprise production, Weber posed the question of why, in the absence of any economic compulsion, the early capitalist manufacturers persisted in their pursuit of profits far beyond the point at which their own consumption needs had been met. As is well known, he identified a distinctive 'spirit of capitalism' in which the pursuit of gain by the unceasing calculation of net profit had become an end in itself, rather than a means to affording a culturally prescribed style of life. But how did these entrepreneurs make sense of their historically atypical activity? Why, in early capitalism before competition in product markets, did they make profits only to plough them back into the enterprise? Protestantism's distinctive 'ethic', Weber famously concluded, had an 'elective affinity' with the 'capitalistic spirit'. The 'calling' to work and the glorification of God by the good stewardship of his gifts to humanity gave meaning to the relentless calculation and pursuit of profit for the improvement of enterprise, as opposed to mere avarice and greed.

In modern capitalism the compulsion to pursue profits now has a purely structural foundation; that is to say, it is driven by the quest for survival in competitive markets and by the demands of shareholders for dividends. Nowhere is this more evident than in the absolute exigency that consumers' wants are stimulated without limit, lest falling demand triggers a recession and a downward spiral of factory closures, unemployment and ultimately social and political unrest. Marx's 'fetishism of commodities' is now institutionalized in the culture of modern capitalism, and personal identity in modern capitalism is largely achieved by the display of a distinctive pattern of 'lifestyle' of 'conspicuous consumption' However, it has recently been argued that purely materialist incentives fuelled by insatiable consumption demands can never provide sufficient basis for the continued willingness of individuals to participate in the capitalist system. Unbridled hedonism, selfishness and greed can never provide an ethical legitimation for capitalism and, consequently, they will continue to attract critiques of the system.

Paradoxically, this continually stimulates the formulation of new ideological justifications, that is to say, a 'new spirit of capitalism' which emphasises the 'collective benefits defined in terms of a common good' that it is claimed capitalism can produce.

Factors Affecting Aggregate Reserves

There are many factors outside of the Fed's control that influence the level of non-borrowed reserves. They include changes in currency holdings of the public, changes in the Treasury's cash balances at the Fed, checking system float, and foreign central bank transactions. The Fed actively compensates for these variations by adding or draining system reserves as needed to avoid large fluctuations in their market price, i.e. the Fed funds rate. Over time, the growing demand for currency is the largest single factor requiring reserve injections.

The Treasury holds working balances at the Fed for making payments on behalf of the government. Drawing down those balances increases aggregate banking system reserves since it results in a transfer of funds to the banking system.

In order to minimize variations in total banking system reserves due to its own spending, the Treasury targets a fixed balance of $5 billion at the Fed by transferring funds as required from its Treasury Tax & Loan accounts at commercial banks. TT&L accounts serve as collection points for receipts from taxes and the sale of securities, and are reserves of the banking system.

Many foreign central banks keep working balances at the Fed to execute their dollar-denominated transactions. Drawing down of those balances increases the reserves of depository institutions receiving payments. Transfers can sometimes result in significant increases or decreases in reserves, requiring offsetting open market operations by the Fed.

How the Fed Manages Reserves

The Fed adjusts aggregate banking system reserves through short term transactions with security dealers, primarily repurchase agreements involving Treasury debt. Occasionally the Fed purchases Treasury debt outright, which then becomes a permanent addition to the monetary base. If necessary the Fed could sell Treasury debt from its portfolio, but that seldom happens in a growing economy.

Size and Composition of the Monetary Base

As of July 2006, the monetary base created by the Fed totaled $812 billion. Of that total, $767 billion consisted of Federal Reserve notes and coins held by the public. The Fed estimates that more than half of the currency is overseas, mostly owned by foreigners. Federal Reserve notes are prized as a store of value and used as a medium of exchange in those countries where the local currency is not trusted.

The remainder of the monetary base comprises the reserves of depository institutions (commercial banks and thrifts). Those reserves support a multiple of bank money created through the act of lending.

Linkage Between Reserves and Money Supply

In practice, reserves bear almost no relation to the size of the money supply. Indeed in the 10-year period from July 1996 to July 2006, while the M2 money aggregate increased by 83%, total banking system reserves decreased by 17%. The explanation for this anomaly is due in part to innovative banking. Through the use of overnight sweep accounts, banks can move substantial amounts of deposits out of the reservable category without affecting customer access to their checkable funds.

While this seems to violate the intent of the Fed's reserve requirements, it does not materially affect the implementation of monetary policy. Banks must still attend to their reserve ratios, and hold adequate clearing balances at the Fed. That creates an active money market in Fed funds whose price the Fed can control through its open market operations.

Bank Deposits and Reserves

The monetary base is created by the Fed when it buys securities for its own portfolio. Bank deposits themselves are not base money, rather they are claims on base money. A bank must hold reserves of base money in order to meet its depositors' cash withdrawals and to cover the checks written against their accounts. Reserves comprise a bank's vault cash and what it holds on deposit at the Fed, known as Fed funds. The Fed requires banks to maintain reserves of at least 10% of their demand deposits, averaged over successive 14-day periods.

The Movement of Bank Reserves

When a depositor writes a check against his account, his bank must surrender that amount in reserves to the payee's bank for the check to clear.

Reserves are constantly moving from one bank to another as checks are written and cleared. At the end of the day, some banks will be short of reserves and others long. Banks redistribute reserves among themselves by trading in the Fed funds market. Those long on reserves will normally lend to those short. The annualized interest rate on interbank loans is known as the Fed funds rate, and varies with supply and demand.

The reserve requirement applies only to the bank's demand deposits, not its term or savings deposits. Thus when a bank depositor converts funds in a demand deposit into a term or savings deposit, he frees up the reserves that were held against the demand deposit.

The bank can then use those reserves in several ways. For example, it can hold them to back further lending, buy interest-earning Treasury securities, or lend them to other banks in the Fed funds market.

Controlling the Fed Funds Rate

The supply of reserves changes whenever base money enters or leaves the banking system. This occurs when the Fed buys or sells securities or when the public deposits or withdraws cash from banks.

The demand for reserves changes whenever total demand deposits change, which occurs when banks increase or decrease aggregate lending. The Fed controls the Fed funds rate by adjusting the supply of reserves to meet the demand at its target interest rate. It does so by adding or draining reserves through its open market operations.

The Fed funds rate effectively sets the upper limit on the cost of reserves to banks, and thus determines the interest rates that banks must charge the public for loans. Bank interest rates influence the demand for loans, and thereby the net amount of bank lending.

That in turn determines the liquidity of the private sector, which is important in terms of aggregate demand and inflationary pressures. The selection and control of the Fed funds rate is the key monetary policy instrument of the Fed.

The Effects of Government Spending

The Fed acts as a depository for the Treasury as well as member banks. All government spending is paid out of the Treasury's account at the Fed.

Whenever the government spends, the Fed debits the Treasury's account and credits the Fed account of the payee's bank. The Treasury replenishes its Fed account with transfers from its commercial bank accounts where it deposits the receipts from taxes, and the sale of its securities.

In order to minimize variations in aggregate banking system reserves, the Treasury maintains a nearly constant balance in its Fed account.

In effect, Treasury payments are simply transfers from its commercial bank accounts to the bank accounts of the public.

Funds move in the reverse direction when the public pays taxes or buys securities from the Treasury.

The Treasury must maintain a positive balance in its commercial bank accounts to avoid having to borrow directly from the Fed. However it has no need for, and does not accumulate, balances in excess of its near-term payment obligations.

On average, government spending does not affect the aggregate bank deposits of the private sector. The Treasury sells or redeems securities as required to balance its inflows against outflows. However short-term variations occur because receipts cannot be synchronized with spending.

Banking system reserves remain essentially unaffected by government spending because the Treasury transfers funds from its commercial bank accounts to replace the funds spent out of its Fed account.

2

CAPITAL REQUIREMENTS OF THE BANK

INTRODUCTION

A bank's capital, also known as equity, is the margin by which creditors are covered if the bank's assets were liquidated. A measure of a bank's financial health is its capital/asset ratio, which is required to be above a prescribed minimum.

Assets and Liabilities

When a bank creates a deposit to fund a loan, its assets and liabilities increase equally, with no increase in equity. That causes its capital ratio to drop. Thus the capital requirement limits the total amount of credit that a bank may issue.

It is important to note that the capital requirement applies to assets while the reserve requirement applies to liabilities. The reserve requirement imposes a lower limit on the amount of reserves a bank must own relative to the demand deposits of its customers.

ROLE OF THE BANK RESERVES

A minimum level of reserves was once regarded as necessary to ensure that a bank could meet the withdrawal of deposits. However experience has shown that a well-run monetary system can operate successfully with no minimum reserve requirements. Examples include the UK, Canada, Australia, and Sweden. It is fair to ask then what purpose such requirements actually serve in the US system.

Adequate Reserves Do Not Imply Solvency

Reserves comprise funds on deposit at the Fed plus vault cash. A bank can hold adequate reserves and still be insolvent if its total assets, including loans and securities, do not cover its liabilities. However a bank in good standing can always borrow in the money market or at the Fed to meet its reserve requirements.

The measure of a bank's solvency is its capital, i.e. assets minus liabilities. The Fed imposes a lower limit on a bank's capital relative to its risk-weighted assets to provide a margin against insolvency. That ratio is what ultimately limits a bank's deposit creation through lending.

The Basic Functions of Reserves

Even with no minimum reserve requirement, banks would still have to hold enough reserves at the Fed to cover the checks written by their depositors, and enough vault cash to meet the demand for currency. The Fed and other clearing banks typically require payment in reserve money which bears no credit risk, rather than direct transfers between private banks which do bear a credit risk.

Other Useful Functions

Reserve requirements in conjunction with an averaging period for reserve maintenance can provide a useful buffer against disturbances in the money market.

For example, if there were an unexpected fall in a bank's reserves early in the maintenance period, the bank could allow its reserves to fall below the required amount temporarily. Later it could hold an excess sufficient to restore the required average level.

In the long run, reserve requirements can also influence the level of bank lending, deposit rates, and the quantity of credit and deposits. The key questions to be decided are: what level of reserves to require, whether they are remunerated (receive interest), and whether they can be averaged over some specified period of days.

The Trend Toward Zero Reserves

Unremunerated reserves are an implicit tax on banks, but it is their customers who ultimately pay. The interest rate a bank charges on loans must reflect its operating costs.

In the U.S., the required reserve ratio is currently set at 10%; no interest is paid on reserve balances; and the averaging period for computing reserves is 14 days. These rules are by no means typical among central banks. Indeed the trend among leading industrial nations has been toward zero reserve systems.

A Zero Reserve System

As an example, Canada imposes no minimum reserve on its banks. Its central bank, the Bank of Canada (BOC), freely lends overnight at its so-called bank rate to ensure that payment orders between banks will clear. That sets an upper limit on overnight rates. It also pays interest on any clearing balances that banks hold at the BOC at a rate 0.5 percentage point below the bank rate. That sets a floor on overnight rates. Volatility in the money market rate is effectively limited to within this operating range.

The BOC target rate is the midpoint of the range. In order to steer the overnight rate toward its target, the BOC conducts open market operations similar to those used by the Fed. To compensate for variations in clearing balances caused by federal government inflows and outflows, on a daily basis the BOC offers to buy or sell government balances at the BOC on an auction basis to a select group of securities dealers.

Is the U.S. Dollar a Special Case?

Whether the U.S. would be better served with a zero reserve system is not a simple issue. An obvious advantage would be the removal of the tax on U.S. banks. That would improve their competitive position world-wide. But the role of the U.S. dollar as the primary world reserve currency must also be considered.

At the typically high level of U.S. dollar transactions, without an adequate cushion of reserves the number and size of bank overdrafts in Fed funds could potentially cause serious problems.

RETAIL PAYMENT SYSTEMS

At the retail level, most transactions use cash, i.e. notes and coins. However checks and plastic cards dominate in dollar volume because they typically involve more expensive purchases.

Cash Payments

Cash is the preferred method for small payments because it is the only one that involves no credit, and therefore no promises. Checks are a form of credit and involve fixed costs that are independent of the amount of the check. Thus checks are seldom used or accepted for very small payments.

Payments by Check

A check is an order to transfer funds from the payer's bank account to the payee's bank. Most small banks do not process checks themselves. Instead they send them either to a correspondent bank, with which they have an arrangement, or to the Fed which also provides that service. Both charge a fee. A check drawn on a bank outside the area of the local clearinghouse generally involves the use of the Fed's clearing facilities.

Float refers to checks in the process of clearing. When the payee deposits the check in his bank, he receives credit the same day for that amount. Until the check is processed through the clearing system, the payer continues to receive credit on his account. Thus float represents an interest-free short term loan to the payer. Credit cards offer a substantially longer float period. The benefit of float to credit card holders is one reason why debit cards have been relatively slow to catch on in the U.S.

Giro Payments

The problem of bad checks is avoided by the giro payment method of transferring ownership of bank deposits. With a check, the payer gives the payment order to the payee. The payee must present the check to either the payer's bank for cash or to his own bank for deposit which will then initiate the clearing process. With a giro payment, the payer sends the payment order directly to his own bank, which then makes payment to the recipient's bank. After the payment has been received, the payee is notified by his bank.

A giro payment cannot bounce because the payer's bank simply will not accept the order if there are insufficient funds to cover it. The giro is not a useful way to pay for unplanned purchases in a store. Its principal use is for regular periodic payments like taxes or utility bills. Paper giro payments are unknown in the U.S.

CAPITAL REQUIREMENTS

In 1989 the U.S. adopted the capital requirements established by the Bank for International Settlements (BIS) in Basel, Switzerland. The minimum capital is specified as a percentage of the risk-weighted assets of the bank. The following table shows the weight assigned to each type of asset.

Asset	Risk Weight
Cash and equivalents	0
Government securities	0
Interbank loans	0.2
Mortgage loans	0.5
Ordinary loans	1.0
Standby letters of credit	1.0

The BIS rules set requirements on two categories of capital, Tier 1 capital and Total capital:

Tier 1 capital is the book value of its stock plus retained earnings. Tier 2 capital is loan-loss reserves plus subordinated debt.

** Total capital is the sum of Tier 1 and Tier 2 capital.

Tier 1 capital must be at least 4% of total risk-weighted assets. Total capital must be at least 8% of total risk-weighted assets.

**Subordinated debt is long term debt that, in case of insolvency, is paid off only after depositors and other creditors have been paid. Thus it can be used like equity to provide those creditors some protection against insolvency.

An Example : Assume a bank has the following assets:

Asset	Amount
Cash and equivalents	$40m
Government securities	$80m
Interbank loans	$100m
Mortgage loans	$200m
Ordinary loans	$300m
Standby letters of credit	$80m

The total risk-weighted assets is 0 x $40m + 0 x $80m + 0.2 x $100m + 0.5 x $200m + 1.0 x $300m + 1.0 x $80m = $500m.

The bank must have Tier 1 capital of at least .04 x $500m = $20m and Total capital of at least .08 x $500m = $40m.

Leverage Requirement

In addition to the BIS capital requirement, the U.S. imposes a separate leverage requirement on banks. This is based on the unweighted sum of all balance sheet assets. Off-balance sheet assets such as standby letters of credit are not counted. The minimum allowable ratio of Tier 1 capital to total assets is 3%. Bank regulators can increase that to as much as 6% depending on the quality of a bank's assets. No leverage requirement is specified for total capital.

In the example above, balance sheet assets total $720m. Assuming the bank must meet a 4% leverage requirement, it must hold Tier 1 assets of at least .04 x $720m = $28.8m. Since that exceeds the $20m BIS Tier 1 capital requirement, the leverage requirement governs.

Meeting the New Standards

If a bank is having difficulty meeting the BIS capital ratio requirements, there are a number of ways for it to increase the ratio. If it is publicly traded, it can issue new stock or sell more subordinated debt. However that may be costly if the bank is in a weak position. Small banks generally do not have the option of selling new stock since most are not publicly traded.

If the bank cannot increase its equity, it can reduce its assets to improve the capital ratio. However shrinking the balance sheet is not attractive because it hurts profitability. Another option is to seek a merger with a stronger bank.

Updating the Requirements

Since the BIS capital adequacy requirements were defined and adopted in 1989, banking has become far more complex. The BIS has been working to better assess the risks in the various assets that banks hold. While the basic methodology of limiting a bank's risk-weighted assets relative to its capital will be retained, more categories and revised weightings are now proposed. How soon these revisions will be universally accepted however is difficult to predict.

Bank Lending and Reserves

The following scenario illustrates how the reserve ratio requirement relates to bank lending. Suppose a bank has $100,000,000** in demand deposits and $10,000,000 in reserves, which is just enough to meet the reserve ratio of 10%. The bank plans to issue mortgage loans totaling $5,000,000 for a new housing development. Can it do so before it acquires more reserves? [** The reserve ratio required for that amount of demand deposits is somewhat less than 10%, but we use that figure to keep the arithmetic simple.]

Capital Adequacy Requirement

A bank's lending is ultimately limited by the amount of its own capital (assets minus liabilities). The capital adequacy rule requires that the ratio of its capital to risk-weighted assets be at least 8%. Mortgage loans have a risk weighting of 0.5 in contrast to ordinary loans which have a risk weighting of 1.0. Since the bank plans to expand its balance sheet by $5,000,000, it must have excess capital of at least $5,000,000 x 0.5 x .08 = $200,000. We will assume the bank satisfies this requirement.

Borrowing Reserves when Needed

Assume the first loan is for $1,000,000. The immediate effect of the loan is to increase the bank's assets and liabilities by that amount, without affecting its reserves or capital. When the borrower spends the $1,000,000, if the proceeds are deposited in other banks, the lending bank loses that much in reserves to other banks but it no longer has that deposit liability. However the bank's original demand deposits of $100,000,000 have not changed, and they are now backed by only $9,000,000 in reserves. The bank must therefore acquire $1,000,000 more in reserves to meet the 10% reserve requirement.

Other banks now have $1,000,000 in new deposit liabilities, as well as new reserves of the same amount. Since they only need $100,000 of those reserves to back their new deposits, they could use the remaining $900,000 to back additional lending of their own. But let's assume they have no good lending opportunities at the time, and therefore offer to lend the excess reserves in the Fed funds market. The lending bank could borrow the excess reserves, which would still leave it $100,000 short of what it needs. Where will the extra funds come from?

How the Fed Responds

Other things equal, aggregate demand deposits of the banking system have increased by $1,000,000, but aggregate reserves remain unchanged. The banking system will thus be short $100,000 of what is needed for all banks to meet their reserve requirements. This shortage applies upward pressure on the Fed funds rate, which will bring a response from the Fed's open market operation.

The Fed will purchase $100,000 of Treasury securities from the public, thereby injecting what is needed to restore the balance and hold the Fed funds rate on target. The full $1,000,000 that the bank needs will therefore be available to borrow in the Fed funds market, and at an interest rate close to the target Fed funds rate. Of course the actual scenario is not as neat and precise as this, but we are only seeking to understand the principle.

Issuing the Remaining Loans

This process can be repeated with other borrowers to issue the $5,000,000 in new mortgage loans. The Fed will then have added $500,000 to banking system reserves on its own initiative. At no time has the reserve requirement been a constraint on the bank's lending. Assuming it has a good credit rating, the bank can borrow the reserves as needed. Indeed it can do so after each loan has been issued because reserves are figured as the average over successive fourteen day periods. That allows a bank to be short of reserves on any given day.

Maintaining Control of the Fed funds rate

We have assumed that the money loaned by the bank and spent by the borrowers has all remained in demand deposits around the banking system.

If instead some of that money gets parked in savings or term deposits for which reserves are not required, the banking system would likely have more reserves than it needed and would offer them in the Fed funds market. In order to hold the Fed funds rate on target, the Fed would need to drain the excess reserves. It would do so by selling Treasury securities from its own portfolio.

Note that the whole system revolves around what must be done to control the Fed funds rate, the primary monetary policy tool of the Fed. The Fed funds rate sets the upper limit on the cost to banks of borrowed funds, which in turn determines the interest rate banks charge on loans to the public.

NON-BANKS VERSUS BANKS

Banks play a key role in the monetary system, yet their lending now accounts for less than 20% of the total credit market debt in the U.S. Most of the lending is done by non-bank financial institutions such as finance companies, mortgage companies, insurance companies, pension funds, and investment banks. Non-banks cannot accept demand deposits, and therefore play no direct role in the payment system. But they provide a variety of financial products and compete with banks and each other for lending opportunities.

Non-Bank Lending

Non-banks are ordinary intermediaries. They act as a conduit between those with funds to lend and those in need of funds. By pooling the funds of investors from whom they borrow, they can then lend in various amounts and periods. For their service they charge a fee, usually in the form of periodic interest payments. Their borrowing and lending increases the total credit market debt but has no direct effect on the money supply. Non-banks simply intermediate the transfer of funds from the bank accounts of the original investors to the bank accounts of the ultimate borrowers.

Non-banks usually borrow short-term at lower rates to lend longer term at higher rates. That means a non-bank must be able to roll over its short-term debt at favorable rates. It must also be able to borrow on short notice to manage any cash flow problem. For that reason it must maintain an excellent credit rating, or it may not be able to borrow at all.

Bank Lending

Banks are not ordinary intermediaries. Like non-banks, they also borrow, but they do not lend the deposits they acquire. They lend by crediting the borrower's account with a new deposit, and then if necessary borrowing the funds needed to meet the reserve ratio requirement. The accounts of other depositors remain intact and their deposits fully available for withdrawal. Thus a bank loan increases the total of bank deposits, which means an increase in the money supply. When the loan is paid off, the money supply decreases.

A net increase in bank lending results in a shortage of reserves needed by the banking system, which only the Fed can supply. In order to maintain control of the Fed funds rate, i.e.

the interest rate on overnight loans between banks, the Fed must provide the funds as required. It does so by purchasing Treasury securities from the public.

Bank lending has no effect on a bank's own capital. But bank lending is limited by the capital ratio requirement set by the Fed. If a bank has sufficient capital, it can expand its balance sheet by issuing more loans. However if it is not holding excess reserves, it will have to acquire more in order to meet the reserve ratio requirement. Banks therefore actively seek new deposits. Of course they prefer deposits on which they pay no interest, like ordinary checking accounts. They also borrow from savers who open savings accounts and investors who buy their CDs.

Deposit Insurance and Bank Failures

The following is a digest of the chapter on "Deposit Insurance" in Financial Institutions and Markets by Meir Kohn, McGraw-Hill, 1994.

After a rash of bank failures in the early 1930s, Federal deposit insurance was enacted by Congress, but over strong opposition. The opponents argued that it would encourage bad banking and eventually become a burden to the taxpayer. But for the first time in the history of American banking, there was a lengthy period without bank runs or banking panics, and very few banks failed. That all began to change in the 1970s. It reached a crisis in the 1980s when bank failures, though less numerous, far exceeded the total assets (in constant dollars) of failed banks in the 1930s.

The S&L crisis of the 1980s wiped out the Federal Savings and Loan Insurance Corporation (FSLIC). As a result, Congress revised the system. In 1989 deposit insurance was consolidated under the Federal Deposit Insurance Corporation (FDIC). Two funds were set up, the Bank Insurance Fund (BIF) which covers commercial banks and savings banks, and the Savings Association Insurance Fund (SAIF) which insures deposits at S&Ls. The focus here is on deposit insurance as it relates to banks. Insure banks pay a premium on all their deposits, even those deposits that are not covered by insurance. For many years, premium income exceeded the cost of failures. But as the size of bank failures increased, the BIF went into the red in 1991.

Instead of being declared insolvent, however, its losses were covered with loans from the Treasury, as authorized by Congress. In 1992 the fund staged a comeback. With increased premiums and a sharp improvement in bank profitability due to a drop in the interest rates, the BIF repaid its loans and was well in the black again by mid-1993.

Dealing with Bank Failure

A bank is insolvent when its liabilities exceed its assets. The FDIC monitors the banks that it insures, but the authority to close a bank rests with whoever gave it a charter. Once an insolvent bank is closed, there are three ways for the FDIC to proceed. They are (1) a payout, (2) a purchase and assumption, or (3) a bridge bank. We will examine each of these options.

Payout

In a payout, the insolvent bank is liquidated and ceases to exist. The FDIC pays off its insured depositors. It then sells the bank's assets and uses the proceeds to pay off the bank's creditors. These include the owners of uninsured deposits and the FDIC itself. The FDIC becomes a creditor by purchasing the insured deposits. The creditors share pro rata in whatever proceeds are realized from the liquidation.

Purchase and Assumption

In a purchase and assumption (P&A), the FDIC arranges for another bank to purchase the failed bank and to assume it liabilities. Banks interested submit bids in an auction process. There are two versions of P&A. In a clean-bank P&A, the successful bidder takes over the liabilities but not the assets. The FDIC pays the bank the cash value of the liabilities less the amount of the bid. It then liquidates the assets and keeps the proceeds. In a whole-bank P&A, the successful bidder takes over the assets as well as the liabilities. The FDIC pays it the value of the liabilities less the market value of the assets, less the amount of the bid. The net cost to the FDIC is the same in both versions, but the whole-bank version ties up less of its resources because it does not have to take on and liquidate the loans. As the amount of the assets the FDIC has under liquidation has soared, it has increasingly leaned toward the whole-bank version.

Bridge Bank

In the bridge bank option, the FDIC replaces the board of directors of the insolvent bank and provides whatever capital is required to reorganize it and get it running properly. In exchange, the FDIC receives an equity stake in the bank. While under the wing of the FDIC, the bank is known as a 'bridge bank' which continues until a P&A can be arranged or the bank returns to profitability. In this version, not only are the liabilities covered, but the original owners may even come away with something.

FDIC Preferences Regarding Bank Failure

During most of its history, the FDIC has shown a preference for the P&A option. Of the 1813 insured banks that failed between 1934 and 1990, only 552 were payouts. Of the 169 banks that failed in 1990, 20 were payouts, 148 were P&As, and only one involved a bridge bank.

A payout is generally the least expensive for the FDIC because the lost value of the failed bank's "franchise" is usually less than its uninsured liabilities. In a P&A, all liabilities of the failed bank are covered - both insured and uninsured deposits as well as non-deposit liabilities such as Fed funds bought. Cost however is not the main consideration. If the FDIC believes that liquidation and its consequent losses to uninsured depositors and creditors would shake public confidence in the banking system, it may elect to bear the greater cost of a P&A.

The Moral Hazard Problem

The purpose of deposit insurance is to protect the banking system by eliminating bank runs. If all deposits were insured, the likelihood of bank runs would indeed be greatly reduced. But that would also increase the moral hazard leading to riskier banking practice and outright failures. This dilemma has no easy solution.

Y2K and Bank Reserves

The Y2K problem involving legacy software that used the 2-digit format to record the year in dates before 2000 is now a thing of the past. But the threat to our financial system, which is highly dependent, on computers was real enough.

The Threat

Banks normally hold reserves amounting to a small fraction of their deposit liabilities. In early 1999 commercial banks in the aggregate held about $40 billion in reserves to cover checking deposits that totaled over $600 billion.

In anticipation of a demand from the public for a large increase in cash holdings in late 1999, the Fed increased its own stockpile of notes to about $200 billion to be made available to banks as needed.

Even if the public drew down their bank deposits for cash by only one-fifth of that amount, it would have depleted the entire reserves of the banking system.

Obviously something had to be done or the interbank lending rate, i.e. the Fed funds rate, would have soared as banks scrambled for reserves. Many banks would have simply been unable to cover the demand for cash withdrawals. Here is essentially what the Fed did in order to avoid the problem.

The Fed's Response

The Fed purchased securities from banks and other financial institutions as required to supply the needed banking system reserves. By meeting the demand as fast as it arose, it kept the supply and demand in balance at its target Fed funds rate. Aggregate reserves were thus held relatively unchanged even as the monetary base increased by the amount of cash actually withdrawn, about $40 billion.

After the smoke cleared in early 2000, people returned the unneeded cash into their bank accounts. That would have flooded banks with excess reserves and caused the Fed funds rate to collapse. However the Fed sold securities from its own portfolio, to soak up the excess. Again it did so as fast as necessary to stabilize the Fed funds rate. The monetary base shrunk accordingly.

What Really Controls the Monetary Base

The details of what happened are somewhat more complex than described here, but the effects on the monetary base were real. Whether banks provide cash to depositors or make loans to borrowers, the decisions of the public determines the need for banking system reserves, and therefore the amount that must be supplied by the Fed. If the Fed failed to do so, it would lose control of the Fed funds rate, the benchmark for all short-term interest rates. More importantly, the loss of liquidity would endanger the payment system itself in which the banks play a central role. That is not an acceptable option.

PLASTIC CARDS

Plastic cards had their origin in store credit cards. Retailers would often extend credit to favored customers, allowing them to charge their purchases and settle up at the end of the month with a single payment. The retailer accepted the risk of default. As the number of customers who bought on credit increased, retailers issued identity cards which evolved into store credit cards.

Later, the financial system developed the third-party credit card, expanding the use of credit to a wider base. The retailer would receive immediate payment from the issuer, less a discount. The cards were accepted only at any retailers agreeing to the arrangement. The card holder would be sent a bill at the end of the month by the issuer for all of his purchases. Third-party cards did not generally offer the option of paying over time. Banks entered this business with third-party cards of their own. However the cards were not widely acceptable because of the restrictions on interstate banking. The banks came up with a solution, the four-party card which involves two banks in each transaction, the cardholder's bank (the issuer of the card) and the retailer's bank.

Charge Cards

With a charge card, you are expected to pay upon receipt of a monthly statement. Nevertheless you do receive a loan up to the date of the payment. Most people write a check to pay off their card bill. The American Express Green Card is the predominant charge card.

Credit Cards

With a credit card, you can pay your charges in full or finance them up to the credit limit that the card issuer has offered you. As with a charge card you get a loan, but you can extend the term of the loan almost indefinitely so long as you make a minimum payment each month. The most widely used is the Citibank Visa card. Because credit cards now play such an important role in the retail economy, a more detailed explanation of how they work is provided in the next article.

Debit Cards

With a debit card, the payment comes right out of your checking account. The card is issued by the entity that holds your money on deposit, probably a bank, but possibly a money market fund. When you present your card, money is transferred from your account to the merchants account that day. The Check Card issued by Bank of America is a typical debit card.

Credit Cards

A credit card is the only form of payment card that offers a revolving line of credit in addition to its function as a means of electronic payment. In contrast, charge cards as offered by American Express must be paid off monthly.

How does a Credit Card Work in Practice?

Suppose you buy a TV and present a Visa card, bearing the logo of the issuer, say Citibank, in payment. You swipe your card through a card reader, which reads the data on the magnetic stripe and adds information that identifies the merchant and the dollar value of the purchase. This electronic message automatically goes via telephone line to a computer maintained by the merchant's acquirer, also a member of the Visa association. That computer reads the message and determines that you used a Visa card. It calls up Visa's computer, which checks with Citibank's computer to verify that you have a credit balance sufficient to cover the purchase.

If you have enough credit, the Citibank computer will send back a message to the Visa computer authorizing the transaction. Visa relays the message back to the terminal at the store. The entire process takes just seconds, and finishes by printing out the credit charge receipt that you must sign. Since the transaction is captured and stored electronically, the receipt is used only to settle disputes that might arise for example due to a stolen card with a forged signature,

The merchant submits a request for payment to its acquirer, which in turn sends it to Visa's computer. The Visa computer passes on the request to Citibank's computer, which posts the transaction to your account with Citibank. Visa's computer consolidates this transaction with all other Visa transactions that day and settles the accounts among banks.

The merchant receives about 2 percent less than the amount you paid for the TV. That 2 percent is called the merchant discount, and is paid to the acquirer.

The acquirer keeps a portion for his services, and pays about 1.4 percent of the purchase amount to the issuer, in this case Citibank. That 1.4 percent is called the interchange fee which is set by Visa. American Express does not have an interchange fee because it is both the issuer and acquirer, and keeps the entire merchant discount.

Credit Card Associations

Visa and MasterCard are by far the largest payment card systems. Visa accounts for more than half of global purchases, with MasterCard ranking second and American Express third.

Surprisingly, neither Visa nor MasterCard earn profits. Both are for-profit corporations, yet they are operated on a break-even basis.

They cover their costs with fees levied on their membership, which totals many thousands of banks. The associations have their own management and employees, but they are owned by the banks that issue their cards, and are supervised by boards of directors composed of representatives of those banks.

A bank can be a member of both associations, but may serve on the board of directors of only one or the other. The daily operations of the two associations are run by separate managements. The following rules apply to the Visa association, but the MasterCard association has similar rules.

The board of directors of an association is elected by the member banks, which are allocated votes based on the volume of various products they offer. The board appoints the management which hires the staff and is responsible for the following:

- Developing operating regulations
- Processing transactions and interchange payments between members.
- Developing system-wide innovations such as interchange technologies.
- Promoting the association brand through advertising.
- Coordinating other system wide matters, such as fraud control.

Individual members, besides being responsible for their own financial commitments, set card interest rates, fees, special features, and sign up card holders (as issuers) and merchants (as acquirers).

Issuers

Card issuers receive revenues from two sources: merchants who accept their cards and consumers who use their cards. Finance charges on credit card loans comprise over three-quarters of the revenues. By comparison, merchant discount fees comprise over half of the revenues on American Express charge cards.

Issuers must properly manage a number of expenses, of which the cost of funds and bad debt charge-offs are the largest. Other expenses include labor, data processing, system development and maintenance, and new card solicitations.

Computerized credit scoring has increased issuers' ability to weed out potential deadbeats, but it remains hard to predict which cardholders will default. The delinquency rate on bankcard loans remains well above that on mortgages, auto loans, and personal loans.

Acquirers

Only members of the association can enter into contracts with merchants, although member banks can work with third-party firms to do so. Acquirers perform the following functions:

- Signing up merchants and managing the relationship
- Installing terminal equipment
- Providing authorization services when customers present their cards
- Keeping track of transactions and reporting the data to merchants
- Transferring funds to the merchant on a daily basis to cover card purchases, i.e. clearing and settlement
- Responding to merchant problems with card processing

Some acquiring banks conduct all aspects of merchant acquiring, from signing up the merchant to transaction processing and customer service.

Other banks serve as the customer's point of contact but outsource the processing functions to third parties. Still others serve only as the depository institution where clearing and settlement occurs, leaving the third party as the active member of the merchant relationship.

Visa Membership

Any financial institution eligible for FDIC insurance is eligible for Visa membership. This now includes financial institutions owned by or affiliated with nonbanks such as retailers, investment firms, insurance companies, and automakers. However companies issuing cards that compete directly with Visa, namely Discover and American Express, are precluded from issuing Visa cards.

To become a member of the Visa association, an institution must pay an initial service fee that depends on the type of membership applied for, the type of cards to be issued, and the number of accounts. However the membership fee is trivial relative to the typical revenues from bankcard operations.

Credit Card Loans

Credit card loans have higher interest rates than most other consumer loan rates, due mainly to loan defaults, overhead, and the cost of financing the loans. Unlike most other consumer loans, credit card loans are not secured by assets that could be seized if the consumer defaulted.

In addition a card holder is more inclined to use the full line of credit when his financial situation worsens - precisely the riskiest time for a creditor.

Credit card loans usually include other costly benefits such as frequent flier miles, purchase guarantees, and insurance. About 40 percent of credit card holders use them only as payment devices and pay off their short-term loans before the issuer charges interest.

In spite of these expenses, credit cards are an important profit center for most issuers.

WHOLESALE PAYMENT SYSTEMS

Large value transfers of funds are usually done over systems about which most citizens are unaware and few have direct contact. These systems are used to move enormous dollar amounts daily by electronic means.

Fedwire

The Fedwire funds transfer system is a real-time gross settlement system in which about 8,500 depository institutions initiate transfers of funds that are immediate, final, and irrevocable when processed. Depository institutions that maintain a reserve or clearing account with a Federal Reserve Bank may use Fedwire to send payments to, or receive payments from, other account holders directly.

Depository institutions use Fedwire to handle large-value, time-critical payments, such as payments for the settlement of interbank purchases and sales of federal funds; the purchase, sale, and financing of securities transactions; the disbursement or repayment of loans; and the settlement of real estate transactions

CHIPS

The Clearing House Interbank Payment System (CHIPS) is the electronic equivalent of payment by check. As of April 2008 this system linked 46 banks with branches in New York to a central computer, clearing and settling about 350,000 transactions per day with an average total value in excess of $2 trillion. Most payments over CHIPS are related to the foreign exchange and Eurodollar markets.

As an example, suppose a British bank needs to pay a French bank $100 million in U.S. dollars. The British bank executes the payment through its branch in New York if it has one, or through a New York bank with which it has a deposit. The payment is made over CHIPS to the New York branch of the French bank if it has one, or to a New York bank at which it has a deposit.

As with the check clearing process, payments are netted to minimize the amounts needed to settle. The CHIPS computer keeps track of each bank's net position relative to all other banks on the system.

At 4:30 PM each day, the CHIPS computer sends each bank a summary of its payments for the day and its final net position. Each bank with a net debt must transfer funds to a special account at the Fed. At 6:00 PM, banks that are owed money receive payment out of the special account.

As with a checking account, there is a danger that a bank may not have sufficient funds to settle at the end of the day. If that happens, all banks to which it owes money would remain unpaid. Strict rules are imposed on the participating banks to minimize this possibility. If a bank does fail during the day, CHIPS has a loss sharing arrangement in which the other banks must cover the failed bank's debt in proportion to each bank's credit limit to the failed bank.

Automated Clearing Houses (ACHs)

Fedwire and CHIPS are on-line systems on which payments can be executed immediately. ACHs are a slower but less expensive method of electronic payment. Payroll payments are usually handled that way. The data is sent to an ACH, together with information from other banks. Payment instructions are passed on, and payments to and from the various banks are netted. Settlement of net positions is made over Fedwire.

ACHs handle both credit transfers and debit transfers. Credit transfers are similar in nature to giro payments, e.g. direct deposits to your bank account. Debit transfers are similar in nature to checks, e.g. authorizing your insurance agency to take monthly payments from your bank deposit. In the U.S. most ACHs are operated by the Fed, although there are private operations too.

OPEN MARKET OPERATIONS

The Fed implements monetary policy by directly influencing short term interest rates. It does this through its control of the interbank lending rate, also known as the Fed funds rate. This involves supplying just enough reserves to meet the demand at its target rate.

The Objective

The Fed supplies reserves to banks through its open market operations (OMO) and its discount window lending. Discount lending now plays a minor role. The principal tool is OMO in which the Fed buys or sells government securities in the secondary market to add or drain banking system reserves.

Normally the objective of OMO is not to effect a net change in reserves; rather it is to counter variations in the total. These variations are caused mainly by changes in the Treasury's cash balances at the Fed, checking system float, foreign central bank transactions, and net cash flows in or out of banks. However as net bank lending varies, the aggregate demand for reserves will vary and require the Fed to adjust the total in order to maintain control of the Fed funds rate.

What is the connection between money, banks, and aggregate credit? When can expansionary monetary policy lead to expanded bank credit? And when can monetary policy help avert bank failures?

We start with a "real" model where all contracts are denominated in goods. A bank is an intermediary, which has special skills that enable it to lend to firms that are hard to collect from. The bank finances these loans by issuing demandable claims. In Diamond and Rajan (2001), we show why such an arrangement allows banks to fund potentially long term projects while allowing investors to consume when needed. Unfortunately, demandable claims expose the banking system to real shocks that create a mismatch between the production of consumption goods and the real amount promised to the depositors.

Even if the shortage of consumption goods, also termed a real "liquidity shortage", is merely due to delay in production and not because of any reduction in the production possibilities of the economy, it can be amplified by the banking system. Banks will cut short long term projects, that is, curtail credit. Banks may fail even if depositors have the most optimistic beliefs possible (unlike, say, in models like Diamond and Dybvig (1983)).

All this is shown in an economy where all contracts, including demand deposits, are denominated in goods. The repayment on deposits is assumed fixed over the next instant and, because of difficulties in contracting, cannot be an explicit function of realizations of individual bank or detailed aggregate conditions. In practice, however, bank deposits and loans typically promise to repay money, not goods -- though deposits are denominated in foreign currencies in some countries, which essentially makes them real from the perspective of that country's citizens. What would happen if deposit contracts were instead nominal, that is, denominated and repayable in domestic currency? Would the system smooth real shocks?

To examine this, we focus on two sources of value for money. First, money, and any maturing government liability, is a claim on the government and may have intrinsic value from the ability of citizens to pay taxes with it. Second, money, specifically currency, facilitates transactions; Some goods may be sold only for cash as in cash-in-advance models (see Clower [1967] and Lucas-Stokey [1987]). Examples are illegal goods like drugs, services that are sold in transactions where the seller seeks to keep his identity hidden from tax authorities, or goods encountered serendipitously where the relative cost of establishing a credit transaction may be too high. Depending on circumstances, the "fiscal" value of money may exceed or be dominated by its "transactions" value.

Suppose now that banks issue nominal deposits. To the extent that the real value of a unit of money falls when the current aggregate supply of goods is low, deposits denominated in money offer banks a natural hedge by adjusting effective real demand to supply. And there are reasons why this might happen - the present value of taxes on production falls if production is delayed so the fiscal value of money falls.

Similarly, it is plausible that transactions fall when aggregate production is delayed so the transactions value of money could also fall. If the quantities of currency and bonds are fixed, the real value required to be paid out on nominal deposits will then fall in consonance with an adverse shock to the supply of goods, reducing the liquidity shortage and its effects on, and via, the banking system.

However, perfect state contingent adjustment of liquidity demand using nominal deposit contracts is a fairly special idealization. More generally, the transactions value of money may have large variation that is independent of aggregate production.1 If so, banks that issue nominal demandable deposits are particularly vulnerable: if cash goods are temporarily cheap (for example, because the supply of money is low relative to available cash goods) banks will be forced to increase interest rates offered on demandable deposits to keep depositors from withdrawing. In turn, this will increase the real repayment obligations of the banks, potentially even causing bank failures. When the value of money is not "well-behaved", far from reducing aggregate real liquidity demand when aggregate supply falls, nominal deposits may actually increase it, exacerbating real liquidity shortages, and reducing credit.

Monetary intervention could play a useful role here by making the value of money correspond better to aggregate real liquidity conditions. By increasing the money supply available for transactions when the transactions demand is high (and by committing to provide monetary support in the future when needed), the monetary authority offsets aberrant monetary or real shocks and keeps the price level stable. This limits depositor incentives to withdraw and the future real repayment obligations of banks.

Banks then will respond by continuing, rather than curtailing, credit to long-term projects, thus increasing aggregate economic activity. Our view of the monetary transmission mechanism could then be termed a version of the bank lending channel view (see Bernanke and Gertler (1995) or Kashyap and Stein (1997) for comprehensive surveys) but with a difference. According to the traditional lending channel view, monetary policy affects bank loan supply, which in turn affects aggregate economic activity.

Three assumptions have been thought to be key to the centrality of banks in the transmission process: (i) binding reserve requirements tie the issuance of bank demand deposits to the availability of reserves (ii) banks cannot substitute between demand deposits and other forms of finance easily so they have to cut down on lending when the central bank curtails reserves (iii) client firms cannot substitute between bank loans and other forms of finance, so they have to cut down on economic activity.

The concern with the traditional view of the bank lending channel is that as reserve requirements have been eliminated for almost all bank liabilities except demand deposits, the argument that banks will find it difficult or expensive to raise alternative forms of financing to demand deposits becomes less persuasive -- see, for example, the critique by Romer and Romer (1990), though see Stein (1998) who argues that demand deposits are still special because they are insured. But there does seem to be strong evidence that monetary policy has effects on bank loan supply (Kashyap, Stein, and Wilcox (1995), Ludvigson (1998)), has greater effect on banks at times when their balance sheets look worse (Gibson (1996)) and has the greatest effect on the policies of the smallest and least liquid banks (Kashyap and Stein (2000)).

In contrast to traditional models of the lending channel, our model does not rely on reserve requirements or on deposit insurance, or even on sticky prices. An expansionary open market operation (buying bonds with money) increases financial liquidity, decreases the real value that banks must pay in the future to retain deposits in the present, which alleviates the real liquidity demands on banks, which then allows them to fund more long-term projects to fruition.

These effects will be most pronounced for constrained banks in bad times. Thus it is perhaps best to term ours the liquidity version of the lending channel of transmission.

AGENTS, ASSETS, ENDOWMENTS, PREFERENCES, TECHNOLOGY

Consider an economy with four types of risk neutral agents: investors, entrepreneurs, bankers, and dealers, a date when contracts are written and five future dates: 0, 1, 2, 3, and 4. Dates 1 and 3 are event rather than calendar dates, and are best assumed close in calendar time to dates 2 and 4 respectively.

There are goods, and financial assets consisting of cash and government bonds. Only investors are initially endowed with resources. Each investor has one unit of good, M0 of cash, and B2 face value of government bonds maturing at date 2. When the bonds mature, the government extinguishes them by repaying their face value in new money or issuing fresh bonds maturing at date 4.

Investors are impatient in that their utility is only the sum of consumption on, or before, date 2. Because all consumption on or before date 2 is perfectly substitutable, we will refer to all such consumption as early consumption. All other agents also get equal utility from consumption after date 2 (late consumption), so their utility is the sum of early and late consumption.

The impatience of investors limits the response of consumption demand to interest rates (equivalently, it limits the substitutability of consumption across time), which is needed for liquidity to matter. Each entrepreneur has a project, which requires the investment of a unit of good before date 0. It produces C in goods at date 2 if the project is early or C at date 4 if the project is delayed and produces late. Alternatively, goods can be stored at a gross real return of 1. We assume that there is a shortage of endowments of goods initially relative to projects that can be invested in. Let the gross real interest rate between date j and date k be rjk and the gross nominal interest rate be ijk .

Projects and the Non-transferability of Skills

The primary friction underlying the model is that those with specific skills cannot commit to using their human capital on behalf of others, that is, they cannot commit to repay all the value they generate to outsiders. Creditors will lend only to the extent that they can compel borrowers to repay -- either by threatening to seize the borrower's assets and generate value with them or by committing to harm the borrower if the borrower defaults.

Specifically, since entrepreneurs have no endowments, they need to borrow to invest. Each entrepreneur has access to a banker who has, or can acquire during the course of lending, knowledge about an alternative, but less effective, way to run the project. The banker's specific knowledge allows him to (make the credible threats that will enable him to) collect C from an entrepreneur whose project just matures. No one else has the knowledge to collect from the entrepreneur. 3 Because the entrepreneur's skills are critical to the project, the project is illiquid in that the entrepreneur can pay at most C of the C that he generates.

Regardless of whether a project is early or late, the banker can also restructure the project at any time to yield c in early consumption goods - intuitively, restructuring implies stopping half finished projects and salvaging all possible goods from them. We assume c 1 C C , (1.1)

Since no one other than the bank has the specific skills to collect from the entrepreneur, the loan to the entrepreneur is also illiquid in that the banker will get less than C if he has to sell the loan before the project matures. Any buyer will realize that the banker will extract a future rent for collecting the loan, and the buyer will reduce the price he pays for the loan accordingly. In fact, bank loans are so dependent on the banker's specific skills for collection that the banker prefers restructuring projects to selling them.4 The illiquidity of both projects and bank loans stems from the inalienability of human capital (see Hart and Moore (1994)).

Given the shortage of endowment relative to projects, competition will force the select few entrepreneurs who get a loan to promise to repay the maximum possible on demand, C, to obtain the loan. This simplifying assumption is relaxed later.

FINANCING BANKS

Since bankers have no resources initially, they have to raise them from investors. But investors have no collection skills (and, consequently, bank loans are worthless in their hands), so how do banks commit to repaying investors? By issuing demand deposits! The demandable nature of deposit contracts introduces a collective action problem for depositors that makes them run to demand repayment whenever they anticipate the banker cannot, or will not, pay the promised amount. Runs destroy the banker's rents. Because depositors are committed to harming the banker if he reneges on his promise to pay, the banker will repay the promised amount on deposits whenever he can.

Deposit financing introduces rigidity into the bank's required repayments. Ex ante, this enables the banker to commit to repay if he can (that is, avoid strategic defaults by passing through whatever he collects to depositors). However, it exposes the bank to destructive runs if he truly cannot pay (it makes non-strategic default more costly): when depositors demand repayment before projects have matured and the bank does not have the means of payment, it will be forced to restructure projects to get c immediately instead of allowing them to mature and generate C.

All banks face a perfectly competitive deposit market where deposits flow freely to any bank that can credibly repay the market clearing rate of return.

Uncertainty

Each bank faces an identical pool of entrepreneurs before date 0. At date 0, the state s is realized and the banks become differentiated. A bank could turn out to be type G with all entrepreneurs having early projects or type B with B,s < 1 entrepreneurs with early projects. The fraction of banks of type G in state s is G,s . In what follows, we will suppress the dependence on the state for notational convenience. Also, instead of introducing the whole model at one go, we will introduce the essential features of the "real' model, leaving the details of money for later.

Timing.

Investors deposit goods in competitive banks in return for claims that make them better off in expectation than storage. Let us start by assuming that banks issue real deposits, that is, each bank offers to repay d0 early consumption goods (or claims of equivalent value) on demand for the resources they get from each identical investor. Banks lend the goods to entrepreneurs in 5 While we have made assumptions here forcing the investor to lend via the bank, we show in Diamond and Rajan (2001) that banks and their fragile liability structures arise endogenously to facilitate the flow of credit from investors with uncertain consumption needs to entrepreneurs who have hard-to-pledge cash flows. If investors lent directly, acquired collection skills, but wanted to consume at an interim date, they would have to sell their loans at a huge discount. Far better to hold demand deposits on a bank and let the bank acquire the collection skills. If the investor wants to consume at an interim date, the bank will repay him and refinance by borrowing from others (early entrepreneurs) who have a surplus. In this way, the bank does not interrupt the late, but valuable, project while also allowing the investor to consume a larger amount when he desires consumption. One might also ask if the entrepreneur can replicate the banker's ability to commit by issuing demand deposits. The answer is no, because the banker's human capital is essential only in making transfers (between the entrepreneur and the depositor) unlike the entrepreneur's human capital, which generates value from the project. Thus the banker can be left without rents by a run but the entrepreneur cannot (see Diamond and Rajan (2001)).

Banks' Maximization Problem after Uncertainty is Revealed

It will be convenient to work on a per project (or equivalently, per investor) basis. It is easy to show that if banks lend any of the real goods they obtain before date 0 to entrepreneurs because the expected return on lending even for a single project dominates the return on storage, they will lend all of them and not store at all (see Diamond and Rajan (2005)).

The constraint (2.2) is simply that the real amount the banker raises should be enough to pay outstanding deposits. On the left hand side of (2.2), the real value of the bank's financial assets is the value of the bank's money and bond holdings in terms of date-2 goods - we will derive expressions for these shortly. The term in square brackets is the value in date-2 consumption goods that the B-type banker obtains from his project loans. The first term is the amount repaid by the B early entrepreneurs whose projects mature at date 2. The second term is the amount obtained by restructuring late projects. The third term is the amount the bank can raise in new deposits against late projects that are allowed to continue without interruption till date 4. Note that r24, the gross real interest rate banks offer on deposits between dates 2 and 4 need not be 1 (unlike 02 r), because initial investors prefer date 2 consumption over date 4 consumption. The banker wants to maximize the present value of his total consumption, which is the residual amount he has left over after paying initial depositors d2. Since d2 is a constant, the banker's objective is simply to maximize the real present value of his assets, the left hand side of (2.2). The solution to the banker's problem is Lemma 1: Let CcR. The banker will restructure no late projects if r24 < R , be indifferent between continuing and restructuring late projects if r24 = R, and prefer restructuring all late projects if r24 > R.

Essentially, R is the implied real rate of return foregone in restructuring late projects, hence the lemma stems from comparing the return with the opportunity or market real rate of return, r24.

As for other agents, the entrepreneur produces in due course if his project is not restructured by the bank. If he produces, he repays the bank. Early entrepreneurs deposit their residual goods (of (1)C) in the B bank at date 2 if it can credibly promise to repay r24 1 or store otherwise. G bankers do likewise with the value left after repaying their depositors

BASIC OPERATIONS

OMO is executed by the Trading Desk of the Federal Reserve Bank of New York, on behalf of the entire Federal Reserve System. The Desk buys securities from government securities dealers who have an established trading relationship with the

Fed. It pays for the securities by sending funds to the dealer's account at its clearing bank, as it takes delivery of the securities at the Fed. This action adds reserves to the banking system. Conversely, when the Fed sells securities to a dealer, it delivers the securities and the account of the dealer is debited. This action drains reserves from the banking system.

Types of Transactions

The Trading Desk most often engages in short-term repurchase agreements (RPs) which are used in situations that call for temporary additions to bank reserves. With RPs, the Desk buys securities from the dealers, who agree to repurchase them at a specified date and at a specified price. When the RPs mature, the added reserves are automatically drained.

If there is a temporary need to drain reserves, the Trading Desk executes reverse RPs with dealers in Treasuries. These transactions involve a contract for immediate sale of Treasury bills to the dealer, with a matching contract for later purchase from the dealer.

The Repo Market

The over-the-counter repo market is now one of the largest and most active sectors in the US money market. Repos are widely used for investing surplus funds short term, or for borrowing short term against collateral. Dealers in securities use repos to manage their liquidity, finance their inventories, and speculate in various ways. The Fed uses repos to manage the aggregate reserves of the banking system.

What are Repos?

Repos, short for repurchase agreements, are contracts for the sale and future repurchase of a financial asset, most often Treasury securities. On the termination date, the seller repurchases the asset at the same price at which he sold it, and pays interest for the use of the funds. Although legally a sequential pair of sales, in effect a repo is a short-term interest-bearing loan against collateral. The annualized rate of interest paid on the loan is known as the repo rate. Repos can be of any duration but are most commonly overnight loans. Repos for longer than overnight are known as term repos. There are also open repos that can be terminated by either side on a day's notice. In common parlance, the seller of securities does a repo and the lender of funds does a reverse. Because money is the more liquid asset, the lender normally receives a margin on the collateral, meaning it is priced below market value, usually by 2 to 5 percent depending on maturity.

The overnight repo rate normally runs slightly below the Fed funds rate for two reasons: First a repo transaction is a secured loan, whereas the sale of Fed funds is an unsecured loan. Second, many who can invest in repos cannot sell Fed funds. Even though the return is modest, overnight lending in the repo market offers several advantages to investors. By rolling overnight repos, they can keep surplus funds invested without losing liquidity or incurring price risk. They also incur very little credit risk because the collateral is always high grade paper.

Repos are not for Small Investors

The largest users of repos and reverses are the dealers in government securities. As of June 2008 there were 20 primary dealers recognized by the Fed, which means they were authorized to bid on newly-issued Treasury securities for resale in the market. Primary dealers must be well-capitalized, and often deal in hundred million dollar chunks. In addition there are several hundred dealers who buy and sell Treasury securities in the secondary market and do repos and reverses in at least one million dollar chunks.

The balance sheet of a government securities dealer is highly leveraged, with assets typically 50 to 100 times its own capital. To finance the inventory, there is a need to obtain repo money in large amounts on a continuing basis. Big suppliers of repo money are money funds, large corporations, state and local governments, and foreign central banks. Generally the alternative of investing in securities that mature in a few months is not attractive by comparison. Even 3-month Treasury bills normally yield less than overnight repos.

Clearing Banks and Dealer Loans

A securities dealer must have an account at a clearing bank to settle his trades. For example, suppose ABC company has $20 million to invest short term. After negotiating the terms with the dealer, ABC has its bank wire $20 million to the clearing bank. On receipt, the clearing bank recovers the funds it loaned the dealer to acquire the securities being sold, plus interest due on the loan. It then transfers the sold securities to a special custodial account in the name of ABC. Since government securities exist as book entries on a computer, this is a trivial operation.

The next morning the dealer repurchases the securities from ABC, pays the overnight interest on the repo, and regains possession of the securities. Assuming a 5% repo rate, the interest due on the $20 million overnight loan would be $2,777.78, which is based on a 360-day year. If both parties agree, the repo could be rolled over instead of paid off, thus providing another day of funds for the dealer and another day of interest for ABC. If the dealer is short on funds needed to repurchase the securities, the clearing bank will advance them with little or no interest if repaid the same day.

Otherwise the bank will charge the dealer interest on the loan and hold the securities as collateral until payment is made. Since dealer loans typically run at least 25 basis points above the Fed funds rate, dealers try to finance as much as they can by borrowing through repos. By rolling over repos day by day, the dealer can finance most of his inventory without resorting to dealer loans. It is sometimes advantageous to repo for a longer period, using a term repo to minimize transaction costs.

Clearing banks charge a fee for executing dealer transactions. They prefer not to issue large dealer loans because it ties up the bank's own reserves at little profit. In truth, there is not enough capacity in all of the clearing banks in New York to provide dealer loans sufficient to cover the financing needs of the large securities dealers.

Matched Books in Repos

A dealer who holds a large position in securities takes a risk in the value of his portfolio from changes in interest rates. Position plays are where the largest profits can be made. However many dealers now run a nearly matched book to minimize market risk. This involves creating offsetting positions in repos and reverses by "reversing in" securities and at the same time "hanging out" identical securities with repos. The dealer earns a profit from the bid-ask spread. Profits can be improved by mismatching maturities between the asset and liability side, but at increasing risk.

As dealers move from simply using repos to finance their positions to using them in running matched books, they become de facto financial intermediaries. In borrowing funds at one rate and relending them at a higher rate, a dealer is operating like a finance company, doing for-profit intermediation.

Foreign Exchange

Payment involving the transfer of bank deposits from the buyer's account to the seller's account is very simple if both buyer and seller share the same bank. The process is only a little more complex when they have different banks if both banks are part of the same clearing system. If the two banks are in different clearing systems, payment is substantially more complex.

A Case of Different Clearing Systems

Consider a U.S. importer who buys a shipment of Swiss watches. Assume the exporter requires payment in francs to his account at a Swiss bank, which of course is in a different clearing system. Normally the importer will go to the foreign exchange desk of his own bank and pay the dollars required to buy the francs as a deposit in a Swiss bank. The details of this transaction are handled by his own bank. A check can then be drawn on the Swiss bank in payment to the exporter. When the exporter deposits the check in his Swiss bank, it will clear in the normal fashion through the Swiss banking system.

Where does the U.S. bank get the Swiss francs to sell to the importer? If the bank is large enough and does business in foreign exchange, it may maintain a deposit of its own at a Swiss bank. If not, it can buy the francs in the interbank market in foreign currencies where the ownership of deposits in different currencies is traded. Small banks may need the services of a correspondent bank that has trading facilities.

Use of a Forward Contract

If the importer's payment is not due for say three months, he can buy a forward contract with his bank for delivery of francs at that time. This locks in the dollar price and thus protects him against changes in the exchange rate before actual payment is required. If the amount were large enough, the bank would hedge its own risk with a currency swap in the foreign exchange market. A currency swap consists of two simultaneous transactions. In this example, one would be the purchase of francs for dollars for immediate delivery in the spot market. The other would be a contract in the forward market allowing the bank to sell francs for dollars at an agreed upon price three months hence. At that time the francs would be delivered as required. The currency swap locks in the exchange rate and thus protects the bank. The bank makes its profit as a markup in the forward contract bought by the importer.

The Foreign Exchange Market

Because so much of world trade is conducted directly in US dollars, foreign exchange between non-U.S. currencies usually involves conversion into and out of U.S. dollars. The foreign exchange market is an international market, active around the clock. London has by far the largest market, followed by New York, Tokyo, and Singapore. Large banks and security dealers maintain trading rooms where they post on computer screens around the world their bid and ask prices for currencies relative to the U.S. dollar. Quotes are offered for both the spot market and the forward market.

Foreign exchange trading has grown rapidly since 1971. That is the year Nixon ended gold backing for the U.S. dollar in international payments, thus leaving the exchange rates of the world's currencies to float at market prices. The volatility of those has rates has increased dramatically since the mid-1970s, creating investment risk as well as opportunities for speculative gain. Foreign exchange trading in support of commerce is now just the tip of the iceberg, probably less than 5% of the total.

MANAGING TREASURY FLOW OF FUNDS

The U.S. Treasury receipts from taxes and the sale of securities now total well over $2,500 billion a year. Almost all of that comes out of the bank deposits of taxpayers. Banks must cover those payments with their own reserves on deposit at the Fed, but bank balances at the Fed total less than $25 billion. How can banks manage such a large flow of funds on so little reserves?

Treasury Tax and Loan Program

The answer is that the Treasury spends on average as much as it receives. Its spending replenishes banking system reserves about as fast as they are used. However there can be significant short-term imbalances between inflows and outflows. Banks would be in trouble if the Treasury made no provision for those imbalances. That is the principal purpose of the Treasury Tax and Loan (TT&L) program.

All tax payments by individuals and businesses go into Treasury accounts at depository institutions called TT&L accounts. Government spending, however, is paid out of the Treasury account at the Federal Reserve. The Treasury must therefore replenish its Fed account with frequent transfers from its TT&L accounts.

Payments deposited in TT&L accounts cause a transfer of reserves within the banking system but do not change the total. However when TT&L deposits are moved to the Treasury's account at the Fed, banking system, reserves decrease accordingly. By targeting a constant balance in its Fed account, nominally $6 billion, the Treasury helps to maintain the reserves of the banking system at a nearly constant level. This is key to enabling the Fed to maintain control of the Fed funds rate, its primary monetary policy tool.

The Role of Depository Institutions

A depository institution can participate in the TT&L program in any of three ways: as a collector, retainer, or investor institution. Collector institutions act as tax collection conduits. They accept tax payments from businesses, and transfer the payments to Treasury accounts at district Federal Reserve Banks.

A retainer institution also accepts tax payments, but retains the payments in an interest-bearing "Main Account" until called for by the Treasury. If the Main Account balance exceeds the institution's balance limit or if it exceeds the collateral value of assets pledged by the institution, the rest is transferred promptly to a Treasury account at the district Federal Reserve Bank.

An investor institution does everything a retainer institution does, and also accepts discretionary investments from the Treasury. Direct investments are credited to the institutions Main Account, and must be collateralized. They pay interest to the Treasury at the weekly average overnight federal funds rate, less 25 basis points.

Tax Collection Methods from Businesses

The taxes paid by businesses consist mainly of witholdings of personal income taxes, corporate income taxes, and social security contributions. The Treasury now uses two mechanisms to collect these taxes: The Paper Tax System (PATAX), and the Electronic Federal Tax Payment System (EFTPS).

In the PATAX system, a business makes federal tax payments by preparing a federal tax deposit coupon and delivers the coupon and the check to its depository institution. Upon receipt, the institution debits the customer's checking account and credits an interest-free Treasury tax collection account. The depository institution must pledge collateral to cover any balances that exceed its insurance coverage. The following day, the balance in the account is transferred to a Federal Reserve bank if the institution is a collector institution, otherwise to the Main Account in the same institution.

A business enrolled in the EFTPS makes a tax payment by authorizing, by telephone or computer, withdrawal of the payment from its account at a participating depository institution on a specified future date. On the payment date, the funds are transmitted to a Treasury account at a Federal Reserve Bank via an automated clearinghouse (ACH) transfer.

If the participating institution is a retainer or investor institution with sufficient free collateral and room under its balance limit to accept additional funds, the payment is immediately routed back to the institution's Main Account. EFTPS was first required for large business taxpayers in the fall of 1996. Subsequently it became mandatory for any business making more than $200,000 in aggregate annual tax payments.

Stabilizing Treasury Balances at the Fed

In July 2000, the Treasury and the Fed implemented the Treasury Investment Program (TIP), a major revamping of the TT&L infrastructure that centralized at the FRB St. Louis many of the functions previously carried out by the individual Federal Reserve Banks. The consolidated functions include tracking Main Account balances, monitoring collateral, and investing and calling Treasury balances. TIP now allows Treasury cash managers to monitor many fund transfers on a nearly real-time basis and thus reduce the errors in maintaining the Treasury balance at the Fed. This in turn reduces the amount of open market operations the Fed must conduct to hold the interbank lending rate (Fed funds rate) on target.

DIRECT VS INDIRECT LENDING

The financial system offers two different ways to lend: (1) direct lending through financial markets, and (2) indirect lending through financial intermediaries, such as banks, finance companies, and mutual funds.

Direct Lending

Direct lending involves the transfer of funds from the ultimate lender to the ultimate borrower, most often through a third party. An example is a private party purchasing the securities issued by a firm. The securities are usually sold to the public through an underwriter, someone who purchases them from the issuer with the intention of reselling them at a profit.

The underwriter negotiates the terms of the contract with the borrower and appoints a trustee, typically a commercial bank, to monitor compliance. Because of the costs involved, the issue of securities makes sense for the borrower only when the amount to be raised is substantial.

If the security is a bond issue, the borrower is obligated to return the principal at maturity and to pay interest during the period of the loan. If the securities are equities, the borrower has no obligation to return the principal, but is expected to pay dividends. What if the lender needs his money back immediately? The only solution is to sell the security in the secondary market. However a secondary market will exist only if someone has created it.

Secondary Markets

There are two types of secondary markets, dealers and brokers. Dealers stand ready to buy or sell from their own inventory at quoted prices, profiting by the markup in those prices. Brokers simply bring buyers and sellers together but do not buy or sell securities. Their profit is normally a commission on the resulting sale. The existence of a good secondary market is of benefit to borrowers as well as lenders. It makes the loans more liquid and therefore more attractive to lenders. A more attractive loan lowers the cost to the borrower.

Indirect Lending

Indirect lending is lending by the ultimate lender to a financial intermediary who pools the funds of many lenders in order to re-lend at a markup over the cost of the funds. The ultimate borrowers are normally unknown to the ultimate lenders. A lender faces less risk in indirect lending because, as a specialist in the field, the intermediary normally has a well-established credit standing. Of course, lower risk usually means less gain for the lender.

Indirect lending generally offers lower cost to the ultimate borrower for small or short-term loans. Most borrowers lack sufficient credit standing to borrow directly.

Borrowers who do have that option may find it cheaper, especially for large sums. In fact it may not even be possible to borrow large sums indirectly through intermediaries. The capacity of the direct financial markets is much larger than that of even the largest intermediaries.

Comparison of Risks

The two types of lenders face different problems with borrowers in financial difficulty. With direct lending, rescheduling a loan is problematic because the relationship is generally at arms length and legalistic. The risks are often unknown to the lender. With indirect lending, the intermediary is usually in a much better position to know whether the problem is permanent or temporary. As the sole lender, the intermediary can alter the terms without having to obtain the agreement of others.

UNDERSTANDING GOVERNMENT DEBT

"Our nation's wealth is being drained drop by drop because our government continues to mount record deficits. The security of our country depends on the fiscal integrity of our government, and we're throwing it away." Senator Warren Rudman.

Warnings like this are commonplace today. The assumption is that the Federal government has limited financial resources and at some point will be unable to service its growing debt, in short that it will become bankrupt. Responsible fiscal policy is viewed as requiring a balanced budget. Individuals and firms can indeed borrow their way into bankruptcy.

There is no such danger for the government when it borrows in the same currency that it creates. In a fiat money system the government has just as much money at its disposal under a budget deficit as with a budget surplus.

When we adopted a monetary base of intrinsically worthless paper money in the mid-20th century, we created a new paradigm that is still widely misunderstood. The imperatives are quite different from those of the earlier gold-based system. The key to maintaining the purchasing power of money is to control the price of credit. That means controlling the cost to banks of acquiring the reserves they need to back their lending. The Fed has the primary responsibility, but the Treasury plays an indispensable role.

Government Money

We can think of "government money" as existing in two forms: the monetary base issued by the Fed, and T-bonds issued by the Treasury. Base money represents immediate purchasing power, while T-bonds represent future purchasing power. T-bonds necessarily pay interest to compensate owners for the delay in purchasing power.

The private sector runs mainly on bank money created by banks when they lend to the public. Banks must hold enough reserves of base money to cover their depositors' transactions. The quantity of reserves varies with the net amount of borrowing, which in turn depends on the interest rate. Since the Fed controls the interest rate, it is ultimately up to the Fed to limit the demand for bank money to what the public can absorb without undue inflationary pressure.

Treasury Operations

The Treasury deposits its receipts from taxes and the sale of its bonds into accounts at commercial banks, known as Treasury Tax and Loan (TT&L) accounts. It spends out of its account at the Fed, and replenishes that account with transfers from its TT&L accounts. To minimize variations in aggregate reserves of commercial banks, the Treasury targets a constant balance in its Fed account.

Thus for all practical purposes, the Treasury spends out of its commercial bank accounts. If Treasury outflows consistently exceeded inflows, the money supply would steadily increase and create unacceptable inflationary pressures. Therefore the Treasury recaptures all of its spending on average. It does so with taxes and the net sale of T-bonds when there is a shortfall in tax revenues. In effect the Treasury pays for its deficit spending by issuing T-bonds rather than base money. That means deficit spending has no net effect on the immediate purchasing power of the private sector.

Tax or Borrow?

The choice between government taxing and borrowing, i.e. fiscal policy, is entirely at the discretion of Congress. That choice has economic consequences which can be either good or bad. Unfortunately fiscal policy is often governed by the belief that deficit spending is ipso facto bad. The real economic consequences are seldom considered in that decision.

Deficits represent no financial risk to either the government or the public. All too often the focus has been on irrelevant accounting issues. Indeed attempts to balance the budget can easily be counterproductive, especially during recessions. Conversely when the economy is sluggish or in recession, deficit spending helps support aggregate demand needed for recovery.

Rolling Over Government Debt

Nothing about government debt requires that it be paid off. Of course individual securities must be redeemed as they mature, but the Treasury can roll over its maturing debt indefinitely. Rolling over means selling new securities to pay for the redemption of maturing securities. This involves no new tax revenues. Treasury securities offer a risk-free, interest-earning alternative to base money spent into circulation by the government. If the private sector has more non-interest-earning base money in the aggregate than it wishes to hold, its only alternative is to buy Treasury securities. Since the Treasury can pay whatever interest rate the market demands, there will always be willing buyers of its securities.

Net Financial Wealth of the Private Sector

T-bonds are valuable assets for the holders. They can readily be sold for money or pledged as collateral for loans. Together with the monetary base created by the Fed, they comprise the net financial wealth of the private sector. By contrast, bank lending cannot change the net financial wealth of the private sector because bank credit is matched by an equal amount of borrower debt.

The value of the T-bonds to the private sector as a whole is in the principal, not in the interest payments they shed. The interest payments are matched by tax revenues, and are therefore a wash in the aggregate. Some fear that as the national debt grows it will create an ever increasing inflation rate. That fear is not supported by the historical record.

The debt/GDP ratio reached an all-time high at the end of World War II, yet the inflation rate during the next two decades averaged only 2%. In the following decade the debt/GDP ratio fell to a long-term low, while the inflation rate averaged about 8%. If there is an upper limit to the debt in terms of its effect on the inflation rate, it has yet to be experienced.

Recycling Money

This article traces money flows within the U.S. We deal with two types of money, base money and bank money, and focus on how they move between the public, the banks, the Fed, and the Treasury.

The public comprises firms and households, which are the producing and consuming sectors of the economy. Banks comprise the depositories which provide payment services as well as financial intermediation for the public.

Base Money

The monetary base is the definitive money of the nation. It exists in two forms (1) notes and coins issued by the Fed, and (2) deposits of banks at the Fed. Both are referred to here as base money, and are interchangeable on demand. The Fed has sole authority for issuing base money. It does so by purchasing Treasury securities for its own portfolio, and crediting the seller's bank with a deposit at the Fed. This is known as monetizing the debt. Conversely when the Fed sells securities, that amount of base money vanishes.

Although base money is not a claim on any Fed assets, it is carried as a liability on the Fed's balance sheet, backed by the financial assets it has purchased. In principle, those assets could include corporate bonds and stocks. In practice, the Fed acquires only Treasury securities because of their liquidity and credit-worthiness. The Fed issues only non-interest-earning liabilities.

Bank Money and Bank Reserves

Banks issue credit when they accept deposits and when they create new deposits to fund loans. A bank checking deposit represents a promise to deliver base money on demand. Since bank deposits can be easily transferred by check or electronic means, they serve as a medium of exchange, and therefore as money. A bank's reserves comprise its vault cash plus its deposit at the Fed, known as Fed funds. Any payment involving the transfer of deposits between banks requires an equal transfer of Fed funds between the respective banks. When one writes a personal check to make a purchase, the bank's account at the Fed is debited to cover the check. That means a bank must have reserves of base money in order to do business. In the special case when the check is deposited in the same bank on which it is drawn, only a transfer of deposits within the bank is involved.

Bank reserves comprise a small fraction of the monetary base, but they play a key role. The Fed adds or drains reserves as required to balance the supply and demand at its target Fed funds rate. Aggregate reserves increase when the Fed buys Treasury securities from the public and decrease when it sells Treasury securities. The public also affects aggregate reserves when it deposits or withdraws cash from banks, causing the Fed to rebalance reserves to compensate for changes in aggregate vault cash.

When the Fed needs to adjust banking system reserves, it deals with a group of financial institutions known as primary dealers comprising banks and securities dealers. It does not concern itself with individual banks needing reserves. Banks short of reserves have to borrow them in the money market or in the Fed funds market from those long on reserves. They can also borrow from the Fed, but only at a penalty rate above the Fed funds target rate.

The Transaction Money Supply

The Fed has defined a measure of the transaction money supply and named it M1. It consists of (1) cash in circulation, (2) travelers checks, and (3) demand deposits at commercial banks, but not the deposits of other banks, the US government, and foreign central banks. Note that the money supply comprises only liabilities of the Fed and the banking system. Reserves are bank assets, and not a part of the money supply. Although cash is the ultimate form of money, by dollar volume it plays a minor role in the economy. Cash and traveler's checks are used mainly as portable money in retail purchases. The largest volume of transactions by far involves the transfer of bank deposits, i.e. bank money.

M1 reflects the demand for liquidity (immediate spending power) by the private sector. The demand increases with inflation and varies with economic conditions. For example, during recessions both firms and households spend less, so they usually move some of their demand deposits into interest-earning savings vehicles like T-bills and CDs.

Of the many factors that influence M1, the most significant is the demand for Federal Reserve notes which has been steadily growing. Most of that demand comes from overseas, but the increasing immigrant population in the US is also an important factor.

As more notes are withdrawn from banks, the Fed must buy more Treasury securities from the public to prevent a drain on banking system reserves. This effect is seen most clearly in the steady growth of Treasury securities in the Fed's portfolio.

Treasury Operations

The Treasury deposits its receipts from taxes and the sale of its securities in commercial bank accounts, known as Treasury Tax and Loan (TT&L) accounts. Like ordinary bank accounts, TT&L accounts are bank money but are not a part of M1 because they are owned by the government.

The Treasury writes checks against its account at the Fed. That injects base money into the banking system, which increases aggregate banking system reserves. However it simultaneously transfers funds from its TT&L accounts to replenish its Fed account, which reduces banking system reserves. By targeting a constant balance in its Fed account, it minimizes disturbances in the aggregate reserves of the banking system, and thereby facilitates the Fed's control of the Fed fund rate. For all practical purposes, the Treasury pays its bills out of its commercial bank accounts.

The Treasury has no use for funds in its TT&L accounts in excess of its near-term payment obligations. On average it matches inflows against outflows by selling or redeeming its securities as required.

In effect, the public pays for those securities with funds received from government deficit spending itself. Thus, except for short-term transients, neither budget deficits nor budget surpluses affect the money supply.

3

FREE BANKING HISTORY AND COMPETITION IN BANKING INDUSTRY

INTRODUCTION

Banking has been more regulated in some times and places than others, and some times and places it has hardly been regulated at all, giving some experiences of more or less free banking.

1. Australia. In the late 19th Century, banking in Australia was subject to little regulation. There were four large banks with over 100 branches each, that together had about half of the banking business, and branch banking and deposit banking were much more advanced than other more regulated countries such as the UK and USA. Banks accepted each other's notes at par. Interest margins were about 4% p.a. In the 1890s a land price crash caused the failure of many smaller banks and building societies.

   Bankruptcy legislation put in place at the time gave bank debtors generous terms they could restructure under, and most of the banks used this as a means to restructure their debts in their favor, even though they didn't really need to. The results was a spate of bank 'failures' that provides another addition to an unfavorable record for government intervention.

2. Switzerland. In the 19th Century several Swiss cantons deregulated banking, allowing free entry and issue of notes. Cantons retained jurisdiction over banking until the enactment of the Federal Banking Law of 1881. The centralisation of note issue reduced the problem of the existence of "a bewildering variety of notes of varying qualities ... at fluctuating exchange rates."
3. Scottish Free Banking. This period lasted between 1716 and 1845. The Bank of Scotland, the original Scottish bank charter and The Royal Bank of Scotland, chartered by England, issued competitive currencies. This resulted in a "currency war" in 1727. The result was a cooperative equilibrium, where both banks agreed to redeem. This area of study has been developed further by Lawrence H. White, in books such as Free Banking in Britain: Theory, Experience and Debate 1800-1845.
4. United States. Between 1837 and 1862, known as the Free Banking Era, only state-chartered banks existed. They could issue bank notes against specie (gold and silver coins) and the states regulated their reserve requirements, interest rates for loans and deposits, the necessary capital ratio. The banking system during this period was notoriously unstable, with many bank failures, and bank notes were discounted depending on the perceived creditworthiness of the issuing bank, that is, there was no single, broadly accepted currency or unit of account. Then, from 1863 to 1913, known as the National Banks Era, state-chartered banks were still operating under a free banking system. Some scholars have found that the system was mostly stable.
5. Sweden. Sweden had two periods of free banking, 1830-60 and 1860-1902. Following a bank crisis in 1857, there was a rise in popular support for private banks and private money issuers (especially Stockholms Enskilda Bank, founded in 1856). A new bank law was adopted by parliament in 1864, deregulating the interest rate. The following decades marked the height of the Swedish

free banking era. After 1874, no new private banks were founded. In 1901, issuing of private money was prohibited. Work on the Swedish free banking era has been done by Per Hortlund and Erik Lakomaa.

There is speculation that with electronic currencies free banking can evolve into Anonymous internet banking. The implications of this for the monetary system are unknown, and much of the rigorous theory in this area has been abandoned for a "wait and see" attitude.

A common feature underlying the emerging markets is the reforms governing the banks and the other financial intermediaries. E.g., in India, regulations governing the banking sector require banks and other financial institutions to operate in a more competitive framework. These regulations were carried out broadly, in two phases. It started with the Debt Recovery Tribunal, set up in 1993.

An important question to be asked is whether emerging economies exhibit more risk taking. The answer to this question lies in finding out the likely departure from optimal investment. In other words, are emerging markets characterized by underinvestment or overinvestment. We model a simple firm - bank relationship in a costly state verification framework (Moore 1993).

Yafeh and Yosha (1996) find empirical support to the above. The lender audits the firm to prevent the later to undertake strategic default (Bolton and Scharfstein, 1995).

The basic structure of our model is as follows: The firm has a project with uncertain returns. The funds raised to undertake the project affects the probability of success. This is the main difference in our model with the other papers in the literature.

In most papers, investments made by the different agents do not affect the incentives for each other to invest. However, in our model, we find that the investment by the bank and the firm, is interdependent. The total capital raised by the firm affects the probability of success. Higher is the investment made, higher is the probability that the project succeeds.

Occurrence of underinvestment with costly monitoring is common in the literature- Gale and Hellwig (1985), Mukherji and Nagarajan (1995), Biais and Casamatta (1999). In these papers, CSV framework leads to underinvestment with the standard debt contract.

The reason being, with costly monitoring to encounter the moral hazard problems, the cost per unit of lending increases. Thus, credit rationing occurs, thereby reducing the aggregate investment in the project.

The frameworks mentioned above differ slightly with each other. However, we obtain that costly monitoring may lead to both underinvestment as well as overinvestment. This is because, investment by the bank and the firm complement each other.

In a recent paper, Mukhopadhyay (2002) reports overinvestment in a framework similar to ours. Our results relating to the capital structure problem confirms some of the existing empirical findings. A significant work has already been done explaining optimal and/or observed leverage ratios across economies. Borio (1990) compares the capital structure of the G-7 countries and conclude that companies in Japan and Continental Europe are more highly levered than the Anglo-American companies.

The reason behind this, he attributes, is the financial structure and systems prevailing in these countries. Similar findings are reported in Berglof (1990).

The reasons again are, the financial systems prevailing in these countries. He asserts that while financing in countries like Japan, Germany, France and Italy are `bank oriented', in USA, UK and Canada, financing is more `market oriented'. Demigurc and Levine (1996) compare the debt equity ratios across various developing and developed nations. They conclude that the more developed the stock markets, higher are the debt equity ratios.

This, is despite of the fact that an improved stock market induces a firm to have more equity. They conclude, that `Firms in countries with underdeveloped stock markets first increase their debt equity ratios as their stock markets develop and subsequently lower it.' Our model corroborates the above findings.

THE MODEL

We consider a simple environment where the economy consists of only two sets of agents, an entrepreneur/ firm F and a bank B .2 The firm owns a project that requires input today to produce output of v tomorrow.

The input, X denotes the aggregate investment in the project provided by the bank and the firm. The project realization is v = {0,V}, where 0 <V < ¥.

Capital is raised either through debt, equity or any combination of both. It is not mandatory for the firm to seek outside finance as we do not assume any funds constraint for the firm. The total investment in the project can be viewed as the fund required to purchase machinery, technology, improved human resources etc. This means that better the quality of these resources, acquired by more investments, higher is the probability that the project succeeds.

Denote XB and XF as the investments by the bank and the firm respectively with XB ,X F ³ 0. Therefore, X = X B + X F . The costs of raising these funds are r(X B) = r .XB for the bank and q(X F) = q.X F for the firm. We shall assume the following about the costs,

A.1: q > r > 0. The costs of raising funds for both the parties are assumed to be linear functions.

Further, it is assumed that the bank can raise funds at a lower cost than the firm. This assumption is not unreasonable, given that the bank can raise funds at a low cost because of its depositors. We denote p as the probability of V occurring.3 Let p(X) be the probability of success. We assume the following about p(X) .

A.2: p(X) =1- e-X . Therefore, the probability of success is, increasing and concave in X. The entrepreneur can finance the project in any of the following three ways. Firstly, she can finance the project entirely through equity, implying X = XF. The project is successful with a probability of p(X F) . In this case, the firm retains the entire cash flow. The second mode of financing is entirely by debt financing. The firm can finance the project by borrowing an amount XB from the bank without contributing any amount herself. The bank will lend X = XB in return for a return (claim) of R from the project. The firm retains the residual V - R amount. Finally, the firm may contribute XF as equity while borrowing XB from the bank. In this case, the project succeeds with a probability of p(XB + XF).

There are three stages. In the first stage, the firm decides whether or not to borrow from the bank. In case, she decides not to borrow, the project is entirely equity financed. If she decides to borrow, she decides the face value of debt.

In the second stage, if the firm borrows from the bank, the investment decisions by the firm and the bank is taken. In the final stage, the actual realization takes place and the project cash flows are distributed among the firm and the bank, with debt having senior claims over equity.

Denote P 0 as the maximum profit to the firm when she does not seek outside financing. The total investment in the project in this case is denoted by X0 . Note from assumptions A.1 and A.2, q X0 = ln V , where ln denotes the natural logarithm. Thus,

q V P 0 =V - q - q.ln ...(1)

An important feature of our model is that, in order to undertake the project, external funding is not compulsory. The firm will borrow from the bank only if it is more profitable than funding the project alone.

EQUILIBRIUM

We now consider debt financing. The bank incurs two kinds of costs. Apart from the capital cost, the bank also incurs an auditing cost. As in Moore (1993), Mukhopadhyay (2002) and others, the lenders have to incur a fixed auditing cost, q , whenever the firm defaults on her debt repayments. By incurring this cost, the lenders can observe the actual realization of the project. We implicitly assume two things.

One, the auditing technology is perfect, i.e., once this cost is incurred, the lending institution knows the true realization accurately and two, the banks monitor whenever the firm defaults. In the event that the firm does not default, the lenders do not audit. These two assumptions together rules out strategic defaults as in Bolton and Scharfstein (1995). Strategic default occurs when the money available to the debtor is sufficient to pay the creditors, but is not paid.

The bank invests positive amounts in the project if and only if the debt is both bounded from below and above. The lending function of the bank is concave. The investment by the bank is highest when, (R = Rmax =V - q(V +q).

While it is easy to appreciate why investment by the bank, initially increases with a rise in R , the reason for its fall as R increases beyond Rmax is not obvious. As R increases, the investment by the firm reduces. This is because, higher face value of debt reduces the residual claims of the firm.

Note, from equation (6), the aggregate investment in the project reduces as R increases. The lower aggregate investment makes the project riskier.

The bank responds to this by lowering its investment.The negative relationship between the debt claims and the bank's investment is similar to the credit rationing results obtained in Gale and Hellwig (1985). However, the driving force behind those results were the role of monitoring costs.

These costs, being dead weight in nature reduces the lenders investment. Credit rationing in our model occurs because, lower equity financing makes the project riskier. The second interesting observation pertains to the relationship between the auditing cost and the face value of debt. We observe that an increase in q decreases R* . This happens because, ceteris paribus, higher auditing costs imply that the bank lower its investment.

The above result throws up an interesting observation. With both parties being risk neutral, and with the firm having higher cost of capital than the bank, it appears that the firm should squeeze maximum investment from the bank. However, the above result indicates that the firm typically settles for a lower investment from the bank than that it could have got. This is because, lower debt increases the residual claim of the firm.

The next result relates the debt level to aggregate investment in the project. Result 2: Ceteris paribus, the bank's investment, increases if either- (a) the monitoring cost, q decreases; or (b) the capital cost of bank, r decreases; or (c) the capital cost of the firm, q increases. Proof: Note that R* decreases as either q or r increases.

As R* £ Rmax , concavity of XB implies that an increase in R* will lead to an increase in * XB . Therefore, an increase q or r which affects R* adversely, will also affect * XB adversely. Part (c) can be established from the fact that an increase in q leads to an increase in R* . .

The above findings are not surprising. The negative impact of q and r on X*B is expected. However, part (c) of the proposition is interesting.

A reduction in equity capital without accompanied by any other measure would reduce the success probability enormously. In order to prevent this from happening, the firm increases the face value of debt. In increase in debt, leads to an increase in the bank's funding.

In a study by Biais and Casamatta (1999), it is established that the optimal leverage ratio decreases with a worsening of the moral hazard problem.

Translated to our model, a severe moral hazard problem due to strategic under reporting, will be tackled by the bank by intensifying its monitoring activities.

This in turn would mean a higher monitoring cost. We predict that the optimal leverage ratio is lower in such a case. In the most recent work of Booth et al (2001), a negative relation is established between agency cost of debt and the debt to book value ratio. They base their studies based on country wise comparisons.

We empirically test the foundation of our model- the fact that increase in investment reduces probability of default.

We test the model using a cross section of rural banks operating in India.7 We have the data for 196 such banks during 2002 and 2003. The data available are on the variables Gross NPA (NPA) and Gross Advances (GRADV).

An important policy implication from the above result comes from the empirical relationship between the relationships of gross advances and percentage NPAs (Non Performing Assets) of various banks in India.

The NPA (as percentage) of gross advances goes down as the gross advances increase. We consider regional rural banks as these banks are characterized by higher average transaction costs. The findings are reported for Regional banks.

With a direct relationship between probability of default and NPAs, this suggest that more investment by the bank increases the success probability. The policy implication that can be drawn from the above is, allowing banks with higher auditing costs, would not be inefficient.

CONCLUSION

In this paper, we model the creditor - borrower relationship in a costly state verification framework. In order to prevent strategic default, auditing by the bank is done only in the default states.

Our model differs from those in the literature with respect to the relationship between the funds raised and the expected profitability of the project. In our model, the amount of funds raised directly influences the success probability of the project. We empirically test the above using data of 196 regional rural banks. We establish that lower auditing costs may lead to uderinvestment while higher auditing costs may lead to overinvestment. The overinvestment result may seen paradoxical, but is explained by the fact that inefficiency in bank lending, is more than offset by an increase in equity.

We also find that, while lending costs to the bank affects the debt equity ratio inversely, the capital cost of the firm affects the ratio directly.

FREE BANKING

Free banking is a theory of banking in which commercial banks and market forces control the provision of banking services.

Under free banking, government central banks and currency boards do not exist, and banking-specific government regulations are either non-existent or not as strict.

Banking services may include bank note issue, cheque accounts, deposit acceptance, and/or money lending.

INSTITUTIONS OF FREE BANKING

Free banking institutionally is:

1. Freedom to form banks
2. Freedom to issue banknotes (promissory notes issued by a bank payable to bearer on demand)
3. Freedom to accept money on deposit to current account, and to pay and collect cheques for customers
4. Freedom to borrow money on term deposit and other forms of secured and unsecured borrowing
5. Freedom to lend money and otherwise invest the bank's assets
6. Freedom to provide guarantees, documentary letters of credit, performance bonds and to incur other off balance sheet exposures.

Characteristics of Free Banking

Free banking theorists consider that free banking is characterised by:

1. Competitive issue of redeemable bearer money. Historically this meant banknotes (promissory notes issued by a bank payable to bearer on demand) issued in the form of paper or metal tokens, but cryptography and modern communications technology mean that it can now take the form of electronic tokens, too.
2. Mutual acceptance by banks of each other's notes at par, and indirect redemption of notes by banks through note exchanges.
3. In the same way competitive provision of current account services, but cooperation, too, in clearing of inter-bank payments between such accounts through clearing houses and settlement banks.
4. Development of short term credit markets to allow banks with excess reserves to invest them at interest, and banks in need of reserves to borrow funds short term.
5. Development of, and bank investment in, marketable debt securities, providing investment opportunities that can be liquidated at short notice, and acting as collateral for short term inter-bank borrowing and lending.

CHARACTERISTICS OF BANKING FIRM AND INDUSTRY

Financial institutions may be defined as economic agents specializing in the activities of buying and selling at the same time financial contracts and securities. Banks may be seen as a subset of the financial institutions, which are retailers of financial securities: they buy the securities issued by borrowers and they sell them to lenders. In view of varied and complex operations of a bank, an operational definition of a bank may be provided as follows. A bank is an institution whose current operations consist in granting loans and receiving deposits from the public. Definition of "Banking" as per the Banking Regulation Act, 1949 says-"banking" means the accepting, for the purpose of lending or investment, of deposits of money from the public, repayable on demand or otherwise, and withdrawable by cheque, draft, order or otherwise". The Act defined the functions that a commercial bank can undertake and restricted their sphere of activities.

Banking theories provide us with insights into why banks exist in the economy. If these theories are correct, banks exist because they perform certain special functions that no other financial services firms can replicate. Thus, no matter what course financial modernization takes in the future, we can count on certain defining characteristics in banking to be preserved. Financial innovation has greatly changed the business of banking. Instead of just accepting deposits and making loans the old-fashioned way, banks nowadays are increasingly active in lending without putting loans on their balance sheets, through either securitization of their asset portfolio or outright loan sales (bonds/debts). Banks also are shifting from interestbased revenues towards fee-based activities, including lines of credit and many types of credit guarantees.

Economists have been asking the question "what's different about banks" for ages. In his famous article, Corrigan (1982) argued that banks are special because: (1) they provide transaction services and administer the nation's payments system; (2) they provide backup liquidity to the economy; and (3) they are transmitters of monetary policy. Based on this argument, what makes banks special spans both the asset side and the liability side of the bank's balance sheet: banks make loans in the course of providing liquidity, and they accept demand deposits in providing transaction services. Since only commercial banks have the unrestricted power to make commercial loans and accept demand deposits, it is their banking power that defines the distinctiveness of banks.

One can go deeper into the distinctiveness of banks and ask a more fundamental question: Why do banks make loans and provide deposit services? For decades, banking researchers have studied the question of why banks exist and have made considerable progress in developing banking theories to explain banks' central role in the economy. Although many of us may take the existence of banks for granted in a "perfect" world, where savers can channel their surplus funds to borrowers without friction, financial intermediaries like banks are not needed. As a corollary, banks' existence must be motivated by certain economic frictions, so that banks, as financial intermediaries, can provide some "value added" from transferring funds from savers to borrowers and providing liquidity.

An important value added provided by banks, according to several theories, is dealing with the information problems in lending and the incentive problems caused by the moral hazard behavior of borrowers. Because a lender must evaluate a borrower's creditworthiness, banks' investments in information technology allow them to achieve scale economies in information production, making them more efficient information producers than individual investors.

Delegating the loan monitoring function to banks avoids the redundancy of monitoring by numerous individual depositors. Banks are credible monitors because their returns are more predictable due to the diversification effect of making a large number of loans (Diamond 1984). With credibility, banks can gather deposits at relatively low cost. While information production represents a key function performed by banks, banks by no means have monopoly access to information production technology.

Other non-bank lenders, such as finance companies, also engage in information production and loan monitoring. Moreover, non-bank lenders could enjoy certain advantages over banks because they are not subject to banking regulations. However, empirical evidence suggests that there is something "special" about bank loans.

Specifically, research has found that bank loan approvals represent positive economic signals that can lift the borrowing firms' stock prices, while loan approval by nonbank lenders does not have the same economic effect (for example, see James 1987). Since loan making by itself does not seem to make banks special, banking theorists also have focused on the role of liquidity provision in conjunction with loan making to explain the unique economic function performed by banks. Calomiris and Kahn (1991), Flannery (1994), and Diamond and Rajan (2001) showed that the fragile capital structure in banks and, hence, their vulnerability to deposit runs serve important economic functions. Deposit runs represent a powerful disciplining device that limits banks' incentives for risk-taking and misallocation of resources. This provides some degree of quality assurance in banks' loan portfolios.

Because nonbank lenders that cannot issue demand deposits do not have the "benefits" of a fragile capital structure, they are less credible in their loan portfolio quality commitment. This may explain why a loan approval by non-bank lenders does not carry the same "good news" weight, as does a loan approval by banks. The same is true for fee-based activities, where banks do not make loans but provide credit lines, credit enhancements, or credit guarantees. Banks can provide these fee-based services because of their credibility, which stems from their commitment to low-risk assets as dictated by their fragile capital structure.

Both securities underwriting and loan making involve pricing financial assets. In loan making, a bank underwrites a loan and then funds it by putting it on its book. In securities underwriting, a bank underwrites a security but quickly turns around and resells it to the public. Securities underwriting involves information production, an expertise that banks already have in making loans. Further, information produced during credit underwriting is potentially reusable for securities underwriting.

Furthermore, to the extent that certain characteristics are unique to banks, such as gathering demand deposits in the course of providing payments services. Unlike other enterprises, a commercial bank cannot afford to have a single objective namely profitability. It is equally important for a commercial bank to maintain liquidity without which it may loose public confidence resulting in a run on the bank.

Thus unlike an ordinary firm; a banking firm always has to negotiate a dual objective function including both profitability as well as liquidity.

A bank is also distinguished from an ordinary firm by virtue of nature of risks it faces. While it is true that existence an intermediary like bank has a net cost advantage relative to direct lending and borrowing, banks face a double-edged risk, one from the side of the lender and other one from the side of the borrower. This is because the equity base of a bank is typically small relative to the liability. A substantial component of liability of a bank consists of its deposits. Apart from current and savings deposits, even term deposits can be subject to premature withdrawal. It faces a withdrawal or liquidity risk when creditors are unwilling to extend or renew their credit to the bank, or they are willing to renew at different terms alone. A default risk arises when the debtors of the bank are not able or willing to meet their obligations to the bank at the agreed upon time. Thus existence of both liquidity and default risk for a bank differentiates it from an ordinary firm.

Unlike a firm, a bank provides a public good in terms of liquidity and means of payment. This implies that the externalities of a bank failure are far greater those emerging from a failure of a firm. Failure of a firm creates hardship for the labour force employed in the firm, not for public in general. The economic and political costs of failure of a large bank may be substantial forcing the governments to bail them out. A recent event related to the Global Trust Bank provides such an example in India.

While there are differences between a bank and a firm there is basic similarity. Just like a firm, a bank also produces value added. Banks borrow money from depositors and lend them to the borrowers, it may be argued that, a production process consisting of a transformation process of inputs into outputs, has not taken place. But it may be pointed out that money lying with the depositors at their homes is not the same as money ready to be used by the borrowers. The process of mobilising deposits and consequent channelising them to the borrowers is production in the technical sense of the word. Hence there is value added even in the case of the single product bank, which is only collecting deposits from surplus spenders and transferring them in the shape of advances to deficit spenders. Thus, a bank produces a value added similarly to a firm. Nevertheless, apart from transferring money from surplus spenders to deficit spenders, a bank provides other kinds of services as well. Financial innovation has greatly changed the business of banking. Instead of just accepting deposits and making loans the old-fashioned way, banks nowadays are increasingly active in lending without putting loans on their balance sheets, through either securitisation of their asset portfolio or outright loan sales (bonds/debts). Banks also are shifting from interest-based revenues towards fee-based activities, under-writing, including lines of credit and many types of credit guarantees.

There is a basic contradiction between deregulation and competition in the case of banking industry. The above contradiction may be established from certain basic characteristics of banking industry as well. As far as the functions of the central bank are concerned, a distinction is made between general monetary policy and specific measures directed to banks. This dual role forms the basis of quantitative and qualitative credit control by central banks. While quantitative credit control regulates the supply of credit, selective credit control, amongst other things, regulates demand for credit.

If rate of interest in banking industry may be compared with price in the context of industry, then control on bank rate by central bank is akin to price control. In a very broad sense, therefore, banks would be reduced to price takers. Thus, in all the three aspects of credit market, captured by supply, demand and price determination, the link between credit control and control of competition is manifested.

A certain amount of control appears to be necessary to ensure that no unwarranted exit takes place in banking industry. Unlike any other enterprise, which can exist with a central control, a bank cannot. There has to be a central bank in order to closely monitor the operations of banks in trouble, provide guidance, and even to bail them out by acting as a lender of the last resort. Exploration of nature of a banking firm establishes that existence of commercial bank is possible only with presence of a central bank. It is important to understand the content of deregulation in banking industry despite the existence of a central bank. It appears that deregulation in the context of banking industry does not tantamount to ushering of unfettered competition. An interpretation of deregulation in banking as pure competition or laissez faire would result in an anarchic situation.

Narasimham Committee which was the main policy document for ushering in de-regulation in banking industry in India recommendations of do not question the basic function of central bank, more particularly, the function of lender of the last resort. On the other hand, it is sometimes being felt that even this basic function can be dispensed with, in favor of capital adequacy norm. The issue at hand is as to whether complete deregulation in banking is justified to the extent that the basic role of central bank is done away with.

An analysis of the banks must be preceded by a clarification of certain basic concepts, like a banking market, so as to provide out the contours of the study. Gibson's (1984) survey of literature on bank market structure and competition highlighted the significance of defining a banking market. According to Haslem (1985), specification of banking products i.e. services and definition of geographic pattern of banking markets are the two basic problems in defining a banking market. He goes on to argue that existence of one single market for banking services, or different markets for various banking services, depends on whether, financial services provided by bank, are complementary to one another, or each banking service constitute a distinct product. The relevant clue to the problem is whether consumers consider nonidentical financial services substitutes for one another or complementary services consumed together. Haslem argued that the determination of geographic markets is a function of the specification of financial services. In the present context, the importance of the aspect of geographical spread of the market is diluted with emergence of telephone banking, Internet banking and ATMs, which enable countrywide access to banking services.

Haslem did not elaborate all aspects of a banking market. Apparently, three factors are relevant in understanding the concept of a banking market. They are a) nature of the products produced by a bank; b) size of bank; c) size of banking market. It may be argued that the volume of both its deposits and advances may capture size of a bank. Such a conceptualisation is derived from the basic functions of a bank and depicts the control of the bank over the market. Provision of advances justifies deposit mobilization, on the one hand, and deposits once mobilised are of no use, if advances are not made from these deposits. If deposits expand but advances do not, profitable operation of the bank will be adversely effected. In a reverse situation, where advances go on increasing but deposits do not, there would occur a situation where the bank will neither be able to sustain increased credit, nor maintain liquidity. In both the situation, the existence of a bank will be endangered. From the above argument, it is clear that deposits and advances are complements. As for the size of the bank, it would follow that it is the sum total of deposits and advances. By the same token, the size of the market is the sum of the respective sizes of the total number of banks operating in the market. Hereafter, in the rest of the thesis, bank's market structure relates to total deposits and advances.

In this context, it is important to sort out the similarities and differences between the two related concepts, market and industry. This will facilitate a meaningful use of these two concepts throughout the study. Industry features production and is defined by the technology and the materials used in a particular product by the group of suppliers who make it. On the other hand, market features exchange and is defined by the products which compete for the business of a set of buyers. The market may be supplied by imports as well as the domestic industry. For example, Indian automobile market refers to domestic trade in new cars, regardless of where automobiles are produced. This is not so for a service industry like banking, where production and exchange take place simultaneously. Thus, banking market and banking industry will be used interchangeably throughout the study.

APPROACHES TO THE STUDY OF BANKING

The main approaches to the study of banking include Analysis of a bank as a financial institution, and its relationship to economic development. · Study of a bank from the point of view of financial management. ·A monetary economics approach which basically focuses on the relationship between central and commercial bank.

Industrial Organisation Approach

We shall now discuss the above approaches to find out their relevance fro study of competition in banking. The first approach is based on institutional economics and does not provide a framework for studying competition. The second approach relates to the internal management of finances in the case of the individual banking firm. Wherever, we have considered asset management, it is only in relation to industrial dynámics and not as an independent study of finance. The third approach relates to pure theory of fractional reserve banking which treats banks as mere passive entities leading to a mechanical modelling of their responses.

Banks are assumed to acquiesce in supplying whatever quantity of demand deposits is dictated by public's desire for demand deposits on the one hand and the monetary authority's reserve requirements on the other. Clearly, the micro foundations of banking theory were weak. Even the H theory of money supply, which apparently attributes an active role to commercial banks in the endogenous determination of money supply, does not present an explicit model of the banking firm. Gurley and Shaw (1960) and Tobin (1963) observed that the theory of money creation neglected the role of banks as firms. However, early analysis of banks treated it as a mere rational investor operating in an environment characterised by risk or uncertainty and not primarily as a firm. Conceptual difficulties in drawing analogy between a bank and the typical firm in neoclassical analysis led researchers to concentrate on only one specific problem of a bank: allocation of bank's funds among competing stocks of assets This approach is grossly inadequate as it completely neglects the production and cost constraints under which banks operate and the role they play in determining the equilibrium output mix and scale size of a bank.

These three approaches may be to some extent overlapping. While there have been extant studies that are based on other approaches, there have been few detailed investigations into the area of banking in India using industrial organisation approach. The extant approaches to competition in industry in general and banking industry in particular invoke the industrial organisation paradigm with two arguments.

The first is based on price cost margins, (Gerosky (1989), Mueller (1986), Shaffer, (1993)) while the second takes recourse to oligopoly (Molnar-Marton and Horvath, 2007, Uchida and Tsutsui, 2004, Capie and Billings, 2004). In the long run, competitive forces tend to wipe out the margin. In the short run, because of restrictions on entry, the scarcity price creates supernormal profits which act as an incentive for new producers to enter. In the long run, entry would ease out the supply. But once entry takes place and long run equilibrium is established in the industry, then price cost margin is wiped out and it no longer acts as a signal form entry. Therefore, further growth beyond long run industry equilibrium is independent of price.

Under monopolistic competition, the further prognosis of industry is a mere dropping off of inefficient firms to be replaced by new firms. Such an understanding of industry and its growth in the dynamic context is faulted. This conservative approach can not explain the phenomenal growth of industry. It can not be price-led. Needless to say, the industrial organisation approach can not be restricted to short run analysis on the one hand and long run equilibrium on the other hand is incapable of explaining industrial dynamics and growth. Even the extended textbook approach of long run supply curve of industry does not explain the basis of further growth. All that it explains is the long run cost conditions which are usually expected to be a case of rising costs. Anomalously though, under such conditions, the long run supply gets re-linked to rising price.

The long run supply curve of industry is more likely to be facing declining cost rather than increasing cost. The implication is that in the dynamic context, price can not be instrumental in raising the supply in industry. Since basic conditions augment both supply and demand, and both the demand curve and supply curve are rising over time price no longer plays an equilibrating role

The problem with the second approach is still more straightforward. Firstly, the oligopolistic models are usually set in the short run. Therefore they are not aimed at explaining industrial growth and dynamics. The limited dynamics which is inferred related to current output and price. It eludes all issues of entry, which by nature is not incumbent upon oligopolistic markets, and hence all questions of industrial growth. Since the main question of interest in understanding competition in banking industry relate to growth and dynamics arising out of entry, this second approach is not adequate for the purpose. The real question does not pivot on restrictive behaviour because the present study is set in at a time period which augurs for growth in industry rather than any trend towards restriction. The moot question then is as to which is the market form that promotes competition and what is the nature of competition that permits such growth? Which is the theoretical framework that allows such analysis? In as much as oligopolistic models do essentially concentrate on conduct on existing firms; such approaches are faulted in two ways. Firstly, a basic objection to this approach is that it presupposes oligopoly as the market form. Secondly, they do not arise out of a complete framework that spans all dimension of S-C-P.

We are therefore led to believe that the only complete framework that could help in understanding competition in general and in banking in particular is the Structure- Conduct-Performance paradigm. Even here, the three primary dimensions of the S-CP paradigm are not sufficient to explain the phenomenon of competition and growth in banking industry. Unless the basic conditions argument is invoked, we can not explain the phenomenon nor can we reconcile it to the evolved and modern notion of competition.

Basic conditions clearly determine the growth in demand and supply. In the very long run, both demand and supply functions could be upward sloping. They are not equilibrated by price. Therefore, the very instrument of competition called price cost margin is no longer of any great relevance. On the other hand, independent of price, basic conditions create new demand and simultaneously augment supply. Amongst other things, one of the most important basic conditions is technology. It is therefore clear that the long run supply curve of industry is more likely to be facing declining cost rather than increasing cost. The implication is that in the dynamic context, price can not be instrumental in raising the supply in industry. Since basic conditions augment both supply and demand, and both the demand curve and supply curve are rising over time price no longer plays an equilibrating role The source of growth of industry (banking industry) lies in basic conditions. Basic conditions include technology, strucLure of the economy, institutions, availability of substitutes, availability of trained manpower, and public policy and rules. It influences growth of industry by creating new demand and attracting new resources. The change in basic conditions creates different types of externalities - technological and pecuniary. Therefore the sustained growth and dynamics of the industry is not price led. Growth arises out of changing basic conditions and dynamics arises out of sharing the new market created by basic conditions. Hence the prime mover of competition is rivalry among firms to control market share rather than adjustments brought about by the price mechanism.

There are two variants of S-C-P paradigm. One attributes larger market shares of firms to their monopoly power and the other relates it to efficiency. Price is considered to be the main instrument or mechanism for generating efficiency. While price represents static efficiency growth any dynamics are associated with changes in market share. If the market share and ranks change then firms would be under pressure and this would lead to efficiency. Similarly, changing basic conditions create externalities and lead to dynamics. There are differences in the rate, the manner and the efficiency with which firms internalize these externalities. The two versions of SC- P paradigm could be reconciled in the following manner. Market dynamics originates from two sources, namely, rivalry amongst firms for acquiring and retaining market, share on the one hand, and rivalry due to internalization of externalities created by change in basic conditions, on the other hand. A caveat on the analysis of changing basic conditions relates to the Schumpeterian line of argument on evolutionary competition. While apparently Schumpeter also talks of technological progress and growth, it must be understood that his notion of innovation and growth is distinct from the present one. In Schumpeter we have endogenous technical progress generated from within the firm that is supported by monopoly and patents. Our concept of competition goes against monopoly. In our framework technological progress arises outside the individual firms and is incorporated in the basic conditions such that it is available to all firms provided they have the willingness to internalize it. The more efficient and dynamic firms internalize faster and better and thereby can capture a greater market share. In as much as they do it at the cost of other firms this creates rivalry. Efficiency occurs on the rebound.

The impetus to change in industry arises from innovations from the basic conditions which could be due to public policy and the State but is not necessarily so. Such externalities are available to banks with minimal risk as compared to the risk-ridden process of 'creative-destruction'.

Rivalry could arise due to three forces. One, it could be due to new entrants which relates to structure (Deb, 2004). And more often than not to price competition. Two, it relates to conduct and is most often quoted in literature. Third, it arises out of externalities which are captured by basic conditions.

Nuberger (1998) has separated public policy from basic conditions and put it in a separate box. Aspects of public policy including restrictions on entry, size of investment and public monopoly (public sector banks) have mostly been dismantled. This led to a blurring of the box containing public policy in Neuberger's scheme of S-C-P paradigm. Whatever remains of public policy boils down to monetary and prudential controls. The monetary controls involve cash reserve ratio, bank rate, variable reserve ratio etc. While prudential regulations relate to asset classification and income recognition norms and norms related to NPA and capital adequacy ratio. All these may be subsumed under basic conditions which again affect all the three dimensions of S-C-P. Most of monetary controls are general and therefore they can be subsumed under basic conditions because rules are essentially part of basic conditions. Rules include regulations. By this count since most of the regulations would be subsumed under the basic conditions, what remains are specific regulations that relate to specific segment or specific market forms. For instance, antitrust regulations could be applicable only if the market form approached monopoly. The liberalisation of interest rate is across the board. Our point is how efficiently do firms internalise the liberalised policy regime. Efficient firms internalise these changes better and they are adding to efficiency. We have shown that efficiency in the dynamic context implies growth unlike the Austrian world. It is not governed by price which is responsible for static efficiency. However, it must be stated that in profitability alone can not be criterion of efficiency the case of banking. An equally important criterion is stability. Therefore in the dynamic context in banking, efficiency can not be equated with Paretian efficiency which may suffice for any other ordinary market.

The way we envisage the process of competition is through the basic conditions influencing structure, conduct and performance. In fact the source of competition and efficiency arise out of dynamics of basic conditions. By keeping basic conditions constant, we will be constrained to observe only one aspect of competition. Our view of competition would be restricted to inter-firm rivalry. Such rivalry is often explained in extant studies through oligopoly models. The broader view of competition as we envisaged includes the right market structure and competitive conduct along with rivalry for internalising the externalities caused by basic conditions. Last but not the least any notion of competition especially if it is to address growth and dynamics must also account for stability. Some of the new approaches to competition are restricted to rivalry for deposits and loans while some of them touch upon risk. From the above discussion, it becomes clear that there is a need to have comprehensive framework which encompasses all the aspects enlisted above. There is none better than the S-C-P framework including feedbacks with changing basic conditions incorporated in it such that competition can be defined and understood as a process that unfolds from basic conditions up to performance. The market from that defines competition has be set in reference to and captured through the entire S-C-P framework.

As a caveat, it has to noted that this Smithian framework emphasises two notions of competition. The former equilibrates demand and supply, while the later is driven by technology and structure. Our notion veers to the latter. However, the re is a fundamental difference between the two notions. In the Smithian case, structure and technology lead to division of labour (which in turn lowers cost within the firm) and is enabled by a growth in the market. In our case, the logic is precisely the converse. Structure and technology change and so do basic conditions. This enables growth in markets and hence creates the competitive conditions through dynamics. Another difference is that in the Smithian case, the impact of technology and structure influence productivity and allocative efficiency, whereas the change in basic conditions leads to technical efficiency. Most of the extant literature takes a partial view. It either restricts the notion of competition to structure, concentration, entry and monopoly power or to conduct and oligopoly, where the market form is pre supposed. Our approach not only develops the S-C-P framework for establishing the appropriate notion of competition. It also modifies the S-C-P framework suit banking and finally develops the empirics that are necessary to analyse and estimate competition in banking so as to pronounce an overall market form.

Initially having questioned the role of price and price cost margin that acts as an incentive in the competitive market form as well as a barrier to entry under monopoly, we wish to state in finality that it is possible to reconcile the two positions. If in the dynamic context, long run price stabilises price cost margin could still emerge while basic conditions are dynamic and create declining costs. The role of competition and public policy is that it should be directed at allowing price cost margin to act as an incentive rather than a restriction to entry. This process would be successful if the approach to competition in general and banking in particular is promoted by the new concept of entry facilitators which we have identified.

There is a traditional notion that questions the desirability of competition in banking. We believe that their scepticism is misplaced. Entry is likely to jeopardise minimum scale only if we assume a context market size. With a dynamically growing market surcharged by dynamic basic conditions and positive public policy, the new entrants would always find enough space in the banking market. At the margin however, if new banks that nevertheless start with a disadvantage edge on the existing banks, this is likely to lead to rivalry and competition, even if there is the fear of failure it has been proven in recent times that such banks choose to merge rather than exit. In fact the new rules that are incorporated in the changing basic conditions permit such merger.

Critical Appraisal of S-C-P Approach

The theoretical framework of the study is provided by theory of industrial organisation. Within the broader industrial organization approach, there are three strands in literature:

- The Structure -Conduct-Performance approach
- The information theoretic approach
- Strategic groups approach

While there are apparent differences between these strands, the focus of all these approaches is to theorize about industry. The broad approach in this thesis is based on S-C-P, while the information theoretic approach has not been broached at all.

The information theoretic approach is relevant to certain issues arising out of the new policy recommendations, nevertheless. The issue of NPAs for instance merits such an approach. For such a treatment of NPAs, one may please refer to Biswas and Deb (2004). While information theoretic approach questions the informational efficiency of the market, S-C-P paradigm takes it for granted and analyses market forms.

On the other hand, the present study revolves around market forms, because the policy framework is directed towards change in the market form. It has introduced a host of measures ranging from interest rate deregulation to allowing entry to mould the market form so that competition and efficiency is generated.

Hence the S-C-P paradigm naturally emerges as the theoretical framework of the study of competition. Instead of simply considering the banking sector as a passive aggregate, as in the standard approach to monetary policy often found in macro textbooks, commercial banks need to be modelled as independent entities that optimally react to their environment. In Industrial economics, a bank, like a firm, is conceptualised as operating under a certain kind of market structure providing a service to its customers and in the process incurs costs in order to produce this service.

In the process, it has to compete with other banks in the industry, using price and non-price instruments and earn a return enough to justify its existence in the industry. Industrial organization framework is a general expression of relationship between the attributes, which seem to characterize an industry. The unit of analysis is market or industry on the one hand or the firm on the other. The framework uses a technique of analysis called partial equilibrium, which is introduced by Marshall. The S-C-P paradigm assumes that certain attributes, designated as basic conditions, are given and a chain of causation logically determines all the other attributes as follows. The basic content of the paradigm is captured by the following few lines. The basic conditions are the primary determinants of the market or industry structure. In the next step, the structure of the industry influences the conduct by participants in the industry. Conduct, in turn influences performance.

Basic conditions

In a discussion of S-C-P paradigm, the phenomenon of basic conditions does not ordinarily receive much attention (Hay and Morris, 1979; Ferguson and Ferguson, 1994). Basic conditions shape market irrespective of market forms. It is determined by the basic conditions of demand and supply. Demand side conditions include: direct and cross-elasticities of demand; market growth in its trend, cyclical and seasonal aspects; taste, requirement and purchasing habit of customers. Supply side conditions include: location and ownership of raw materials; technology; unionisation; product durability; industry history; and the legal, ethical and political framework within which business activity takes place. Gavin Reid (1987) pointed out that many treatments of S-C-P framework assimilate several of these basic determinants into market structure category. For example, Mason (1939) who first proposed and cogently argued the merits of S-C-P approach defines market structure to include all those considerations the seller takes into account in determining his business policies and practice. He would include demand conditions in his list of elements of structure. Whatever, the usual attitude is to regard taste, technology and institutions as given and concentrate structure, conduct and performance.

Structure

The structure of an industry or market is by far the most important, though not sole determinant of business conduct. Therefore an economic analyst cannot adequately describe or fully understand the conduct of a business firm without putting it into the context of the industry's structure. It is important to point out that perfectly contestable markets may also be used as a benchmark for analysis of industry structure. Such markets are open to entry by entrepreneurs who face no disadvantages vis-à-vis incumbent firms and who can exit without loss of any costs that entry requires to be sunk. There are no legal restrictions on market entry and exit and there are no special costs that must be borne by an entrant that do not fall on the incumbent firm as well. In such markets, competitive pressures from potential entrants exercise strong constraints on the conduct of incumbent firms. Hence in a perfectly contestable market, absence of features like sunk costs and entry barriers, structure of an industry is rendered inconsequential for the conduct and performance of the firms operating in that industry. It may be pointed out; contestable markets do not serve as a useful reference point for analysis of banking industry, which is apparently characterised by sunk cost and entry barriers.

Conduct

Conduct is the term used in reference to the behavior of firms in the market. It refers to how firms react to the conditions imposed by market structure and interacts with rivals. In course of interaction with competitors, the firm has to take into account the dependence of other firm's actions on its behavior. Conduct includes a strategic move, which is one that influences the other person's choice, in a manner available to one's self, by affecting other person's expectations on how oneself would behave. In principle, many types of conduct may be distinguished, some of which may be extended beyond the strictly economic. Under conduct, one conventionally looks at: how price is set; the way in which the volume, quality and range of products are determined; advertising and marketing strategy; research and development planning and implementation; and legal tactics.

Performance

Performance is a judgement about the results of market behaviour (Burgess, 1988). The dimensions of market performance about which industrial organisation is concerned include efficiency, fairness and progress. Efficiency involves how well a market makes use of available resources. Fairness involves how equitably market distributes benefits of economic activity to the participants. Progress concerns how effectively the market nurtures and yields better products and production techniques.

ADAPTATION OF INDUSTRIAL ORGAINISATION APPROACH TO BANKING

A number of modifications are made in the standard S-C-P paradigm to adapt it to banking. The adaptation is based on a critical review of different works (Burgess, 1988; Ferguson and Ferguson, 1994; Hay and Morris, 1991; Sawyer, 1981; Baldwin, 1987; Reid, 1987).

In the traditional literature on S-C-P, barriers to entry are attributed to four factors. They are absolute cost disadvantage for entrant, relative cost disadvantage, product differentiation, and large capital requirements for entry. Bain also added the category of high fixed cost to those of absolute and relative cost advantages. Burgess (1988) proposed a scheme of classification of sources of entry barriers. According to Burgess, there are three sources of entry barriers. They arise from natural factors, strategic behaviour and performance.

The current approach provides a more meaningful analysis by an exploration of the answer to the following question: Can each entry barrier proposed by Bain emanate from multiple sources, instead of single source? The approach develops a three-fold classification scheme in which four sources of barriers to entry are distinguished: basic conditions, structure, conduct and performance. It has enhanced our understanding of the sources of entry barriers. The approach established that a particular entry barrier may emanate from multiple sources, instead of only one source, as pointed out by Burgess (1988).

Secondly, the list of standard variables falling under the three categories of structure, conduct and performance is examined in order to develop an appropriate set of variables relevant to the banking industry. A subset of the variables in the original list is retained, while a few new variables, typical of the banking industry are included.

Thirdly, while the role of basic conditions is recognized in S-C-P framework, it plays a limited role therein. Another contribution of the study is an analysis of basic conditions. It is shown that any change in basic condition in terms of technology may directly influence conduct of a firm, bypassing structure. This goes against even the modified S-C-P paradigm, which is characterised by existence of feedbacks. Fourthly, the study has evolved to a new concept of "entry facilitator" as opposed to the concept of entry barrier, present in discussion of S-C-P framework. Traditionally, discussions of entry conditions consist of entry barriers alone, which operate in favour of old firms. However, entry conditions may not be completely described as entry barriers alone. The study points out there are certain factors, which favour new firms, while entering the market. Such factors are termed as "entry facilitators". According to traditional literature related to S-C-P framework, existing firms would possesses a natural advantage in terms of lower cost due to economies of scale, while new entrants could have a higher cost on account of a smaller scale.

On the other hand, new firms may have the potential to enter with new cost saving technologies, while old firms have sunk their investment in old high cost technologies. It would involve a very heavy financial cost to forego the existing technology, apart from the cost of equipment and training.

It could need some organizational reform and may lead to loss of efficiency. There exist certain disadvantages on the part of existing firms rather than to the advantages enjoyed by them, as purported in the traditional literature. On the other hand, the potential for new technology may act as a "facilitator to entry" for the new firms rather than a barrier to entry, protecting the existing firms from entry. It is also pointed out that this phenomenon is not arising out of structure, but out of basic conditions.

Fifthly, the study provides a more meaningful way of interpreting the concept of competition. In terms of the S-C-P paradigm, competition has been classified as a conduct variable. The traditional S-C-P does not take account of the influence of basic conditions, conduct and performance on competition. It is argued in the thesis that competition need not be reduced to conduct alone. It encompasses all the components of S-C-P paradigm: basic conditions, structure, conduct and performance. It is stated that competition is an overall state and describes a market form.

Sixthly, the concept of strategic groups incorporated in S-C-P paradigm. Conduct in the conventional S-C-P paradigm has been conceptualised in a narrow way. The dimension of strategic group needs to be included in S-C-P framework while conceptualizing a broader approach to conduct. In the new framework, conduct of a firm is influenced by its membership of a particular strategic group, apart from the market structure under which it operates. This point needs a detailed analysis. There are two variants of S-C-P paradigm: industry oriented and firm oriented (Mueller, 1986). In the industry variant of the S-C-P paradigm, the focus is on industry. Boundaries are assumed to exist, separating one industry from the other. Barriers are assumed to exist along these boundaries, which impede entry, and may be even the exit, of firms. Within an industry, all firms are treated alike.

A common technology is assumed to exist that leads to a unique average cost function for all firms in the industry. The number of firms in an industry or level of concentration determines the degree of collusion in the industry and thereby average height of prices. Collusion is seen raising a common price umbrella over all firms in the industry. Product differentiation is seen as a characteristic raising the barrier to entry of other firms that benefit all companies in the industry alike. In contrast to this industry approach to market performance, one can envisage an alternative approach that makes the firm the centrepiece of analysis. Firms deliberately seek to mould industrial structure in their favour and influence the behaviour of rivals by their conduct. Firms differ in the products they sell, their organisational form, and internal efficiency. It is the drive to be different that locomotes dynamic competition of the Schumpetarian sort. Those companies successfully differentiating their products or lowering their costs outpace their rivals. In contrast to industry approach, product differentiation is seen as a characteristic that differentiates one firm with an industry from another and thereby leads to different prices and profit levels across firms within an industry. This firm approach to market performance reverses the casual link between size and efficiency. Under the industry approach, an industry's technology dictated scale economies and the size of the firm determines cost. It has low average costs only if it is big enough.

Under the firm approach efficiency determines size. The more efficient companies with superior products grow to be large than other firms. The firm approach to market performance is consistent with the criticisms of the traditional SCP literature by Demstez (1973) and Peltzman (1977), which emphasize firm specific efficiency advantages and with Shepherd (1972), which stress market power advantages.

Our approach does not restrict itself to an industry oriented or to a firm-oriented approach, but adopts an overall approach. While the main focus is on the industry, the approach goes into all three levels: The Firm, The Group and The Industry. The strategic groups approach is usually portrayed as an alternative approach. It looks for strategic grouping of firms within an industry. A strategic group comprises firms, which follow a similar strategy and hence possess similar advantages (Ferguson and Ferguson, 1994). It is argued that the typical cross section study of neoclassical economics becomes less appropriate if individual firms cannot be aggregated meaningfully to strategic groups. Newman (1978) argued that statistical analysis of structure-performance relationship in manufacturing industries invariably assumed that that firms belonging to an industry differ only in their market shares. This assumption is often incorrect. Firms competing in the same market need not choose identical corporate strategies even when they share a common goal of long run profit maximisation. The reasons provided by him include possession of heterogeneous and durable firm-specific asset acquired in a random fashion and heterogeneous buyers' preferences leading to significant differences in non-price attributes of the product produced by them.

Later, Porter (1980) rationalises existence of strategic groups on the basis of a wide variety of reasons. They include firms' differing initial strengths and weaknesses, differing times of entry into the business and historical accidents. In the current study of conduct and performance, the strategic group approach has been incorporated into the S-C-P approach.

Seventhly, our approach provides a framework to analyse competition. Such a framework includes the following elements. Firstly, it is believed that competition is an overall state that describes the nature of the market form. Hence, it encompasses all the aspects of an industry, namely basic conditions, structure, conduct and performance. The figure 1 portrays the idea. Secondly, there is a phenomenon of entry facilitators as opposed to entry barriers. The basic approach to entry barrier does not look at basic conditions. Hence the conclusion that returns to scale constitutes a barrier to entry. Assuming that long run costs are a product of both internal and external economies of scale, it still does not take into account basic conditions.

Our understanding in this context is different from the traditional theory. Once basic conditions like technology are not treated as a parameter but are allowed to change, then it may be seen how it may act as an entry facilitator. It will lead to situation in which long run average cost of new firms will lie at a lower level than the old firms, which initially enjoyed a cost advantage over the new firms. However, it has been observed that in case of banking, change in basic condition directly influences conduct by bypassing structure. Let the discussion begin with the status of old banks on the eve of entry of new banks. They did not start with the provision of having to have an optimal scale in the beginning itself. In the absence of new banks, they got the benefit of serving a whole market and in the process, lowered cost through exploitation of economies of scale.

The entry barrier argument can well be granted in terms of internal economies arising in favour of old firms. These would arise out of indivisibilities and experience. However, internal economies are only likely to enhance the advantage the old banks may be experiencing, in addition to economies that they derive from external economies. External economies arises essentially an expansion of the industry.

In long run industry equilibrium, only efficient firms remained because they have achieved the optimal scale. In the regulated period, the old banks reached economies of scale when they were perhaps producing QMax level of output. Now the issue is how the new banks could enter and overtake the old banks, when the latter were enjoying the benefits of economies of scale.

To explain the scenario after entry with new banks with a better technology, two average cost curves are shown, one above the other. The upper curve represents average cost of the old banks and the lower one shows the cost situation of the new firms. This is because the new banks entered with a better technology, which resulted in lower cost of production. Clearly the new banks enjoyed a potential absolute cost advantage because the new banks at a lower cost can produce the same output.

However, initially the new banks suffered from a relative cost advantage because of a lower volume of production in the initial period.

After entry of new banks, expansion of the industry benefited the old banks in the initial phase. It was natural for people to go to an established bank as opposed to a new bank, which was yet to establish its credibility. Substitution of an old bank with a new bank took place over time, when the new banks were perceived as provider of better services with the help of new technology. However, there was a caveat here. The amount of money needed to open an account with new banks is substantially higher than that of an old bank. Such difference in strategic behaviour limited the scope of substitution of old banks by the new banks.

Thus, it is clear that, the new firms are not likely to have economies of scale during the period immediately after their entry. However, there was a latent demand for a variety of technology-based services emanating from affluent section of the population. In absence of supply of such services, such a section more readily joined the new banks. This caused an expansion of industry in favour of new banks arising out of new technology thus while, technology and new services enabled differential advantage in favour of new banks, and such advantages however would unfold only over a period of time. It was imperative for the new banks to expand production in order to realize the benefits of economies of scale. Their strategy was to target the well off segment of the population through provision of technology based services. With this end in view, they engaged in product differentiation and developed brand names and ultimately went in for merger. In such a situation, the only alternative for the old firms was to go for new technology, which also had its own compulsions. Use of new technology is meaningful only when their economy of scale is exploited. With recession affecting their clients, second rung corporates located in their traditional area of operations, they had no choice but to look for expanded markets in metros. It follows from the above discussion that market dynamics is shaped by three factors.

1. Entry of new banks consequent on deregulation, motivated by expectations of profits through use of new technology and strategic conduct.
2. The mechanism through which new banks could actually circumvent the advantages of old banks included new technology and strategic conduct.
3. Means adopted by the old banks to cope up with the new banks in the new scenario.

An analytical framework to understand competition is developed. Such a framework is based on the understanding that competition is an overall state describing the nature of the market form. Hence, it encompasses all the aspects of an industry, namely basic conditions, structure, conduct and performance. The framework is a product of synthesis of the approaches of S-C-P and strategic groups. While, it includes traditional elements of S-C-P paradigm including entry, economies of scale, product differentiation and price cost margin, it also incorporates basic conditions and strategic groups to analyse the process through which evolution of competition takes place in the market.

The ordinary S-C-P approach does not involve any analysis of market dynamics. Our approach introduces various aspects of industry dynamics. In the extant approaches, wherever, wherever dynamics have been studied, the limitation is that in the case of oligopolistic or duopolistic market forms, firm dynamics coincides with industry dynamics. Therefore, there can not be different methods for studying dynamics at the industry level and the firm level.

Lastly, approaches which start with the assumption of an oligopolistic market structure can not provide a theoretical framework to identify the existing market form in an industry. Our approach provides a methodology to arrive the market form in banking industry through an analysis of the all aspects of basic conditions, structure, conduct and performance.

CONCLUSIONS

There are various approaches to study competition in general and banking in particular. The ordinary Structure-Conduct-Performance approach does not involve any analysis of market dynamics. Our approach introduces various aspects of industry dynamics and growth. It provides a methodology to arrive at the market form in banking industry through an analysis of all the aspects of basic conditions, structure, conduct and performance.

COMPETITION IN BANKING INDUSTRY

Concepts evolve through time and over time they assume different meanings. The concept of competition is no exception. This paper discusses the evolution of the concept of competition in general with a view to derive a theoretical framework for analyzing competition in banking industry. Starting from the classical notions of competition it proceeds to some of the latest approaches (Northcott (2004), Neuberger (1998), Toolsema (2003), Bolt and Tieman (2001)). The ordinary Structure-Conduct-Performance approach does not involve any analysis of market dynamics. Our approach introduces various aspects of industry dynamics and growth. It provides a methodology to arrive at the market form in banking industry through an analysis of all the aspects of basic conditions, structure, conduct and performance. It is argued that sustained growth and dynamics of the industry is not price led. Growth arises out of changing basic conditions and dynamics arises out of sharing the new market created by basic conditions. Hence the prime mover of competition is rivalry among firms to control market share and to internalize externalities rather than adjustments brought about by the price mechanism.

In the industrial organization literature, a tendency to conceptualizes and measures competition by resorting to a simplistic framework. In recent literature, at one end of the spectrum, there are studies like Demstez (19995) that virtually rules out conceptualization and measurement of concept. And at the other end of the spectrum, there are certain studies that seek the convenient position of equating concentration with competition. Concepts evolve through time and over time they assume different meanings.

The concept of competition is no exception. This paper discusses the evolution of the concept of competition in general with a view to derive a theoretical framework for analyzing competition in banking industry. Starting from classical notions of competition it proceeds to some of the latest approaches (Northcott (2004), Neuberger (1998), Toolsema (2003), Bolt and Tieman (2001)).

The extant approaches to competition in industry in general and banking industry in particular invoke the industrial organisation paradigm with two arguments. The first is based on price cost margins, (Gerosky (1989), Mueller (1986), Shaffer, (1993)) while the second takes recourse to oligopoly (Molnar-Marton and Horvath, 2007, Uchida and Tsutsui, 2004, Capie and Billings, 2004).

There are various approaches to study competition in general and banking in particular. The ordinary Structure-Conduct-Performance approach does not involve any analysis of market dynamics. Our approach introduces various aspects of industry dynamics and growth. It provides a methodology to arrive at the market form in banking industry through an analysis of all the aspects of basic conditions, structure, conduct and performance.

EVOLUTION OF THE CONCEPT OF COMPETITION

In the following section we have undertaken a study of the process of evolution of the concept of competition. Such a study would obviously be very vast and cannot be completed in a single paper. Therefore, we have restricted ourselves to gleaning out a notion of competition that is appropriate in the context banking. The following review of the concept seeks to bring out the major elements in the process of evolution of the concept, which deserve a detailed consideration. The literature on competition is vast and so the review had to be selective. It covers the major contributions to the concepts of competition due to Smith (1976), Chamberlain (1933), Schumpeter (1934), Hayek (1948) and Stigler (1995). It also covers some old and new commentaries on the concept including McNulty (1968) and Richardson (1975) on the one hand and Vickers (1995) on the other. A number of attempts have been made since then to develop the concept. However, lack of clarity remains.

But during the process of evolution, the concept got mixed with other entities, and any attempt to understand the true essence of competition has been rendered difficult. There exists a voluminous literature in the area, but the concept remains surrounded by ambiguities and confusions in a large measure. A few reviews of the concept remained confined to only selected interpretations of competition. Some of them also cut across each other. To substantiate the above point an example is cited below.

According to McNulty (1968), there exist two fundamentally distinct interpretations of the concept of competition, which have led to the ambiguity and confusion surrounding the concept of competition. In one interpretation, competition is conceived as a descriptive term characterized by an idealized market structure. In the second interpretation, it has been identified with a force, which through equating prices with marginal costs assures allocative efficiency in the system. According to the first interpretation, competition is a seemingly tranquil equilibrium state in which informed agents treat price parametrically. This is the concept of perfect competition, which is compared to the idea of a perfect vacuum. In the second form, it has been identified with a force, which through equating prices with marginal costs assures allocative efficiency in the system. Through competition resources gravitate towards their most productive use and price is forced to the lowest level to be sustained over the long run. This standpoint views competition as assuring order and stability in the economic world as does the gravitation to the physical world. As opposed to the earlier interpretation, the second interpretation looks at competition as a rivalry with respect to prices.

As opposed to McNulty, Vickers argued that the concepts or competition as an idealized market structure in which price is parametrically given and as a rivalry with respect to prices are not two distinct concepts of competition. He analyzed Cournot and Edgeworth models to show that the notion of perfect competition has its roots in the broad concept of competition as rivalry.

We now set out for a review of the concept of competition. It is clear that the current review cannot but begin with Adam Smith's concept of competition. While Smith's contribution holds a pride of place in any discussion of competition, there are conflicting interpretations of his notion of competition. These interpretations are analyzed in order to understand the true substance of the concept of competition, as understood by Smith. The former commentator has reduced Smith's notion of competition to a process of price competition alone. It is this view of competition as an ordering force, which dominated the classical economics. Adam Smith referred to competition in connection with the forcing of market price to its natural level and lowering of profits to a minimum. The classical view of competition looks at competition as a process for allocating resources to their optimal use through the instrument of price mechanism. When price mechanism functions properly, equilibrium emerges with prices equal to marginal social costs of production. When it does not function properly, equilibrium exists with price above marginal cost. In such a situation, the society suffers a welfare loss from the under consumption of these goods. Such malfunctions are immediately attributed to an insufficient number of buyers or sellers. Monopoly is seen as an antithesis of competition. This view sees competition as a process for determining prices and quantities, the allocation of resources for a given set of tastes and technological opportunities. Competition produces an equilibrium set of prices that induce a Pareto optimal allocation of economy's goods and services. Such equilibrium is anticipated so long as monopolistic elements are absent. There was no systematic association between the idea of competition and market structure in classical economics, which viewed competition as a price determining force operating in market.

The private business firm and the market are the two primary institutions through which resources are organized, transformed and channeled for ultimate consumption as goods and services. Economic goods and services broadly possess two characteristics: quality and price. Firm and market correspond to the two characteristics possessed by economic goods. While quality is related to production and takes place within the business firm, exchange i.e. the determination of economic value, which in is in turn price, arises in the various markets in which the firm operates. But the concept of competition has been usually associated only with exchange, even when economic activity consists of both production and exchange. It is argued that despite according competition a pride of place in economic theory, Adam Smith contributed nothing to its precise economic meaning. The concept of competition, which he incorporated in his Wealth of Nations, was already developed in the then literature by a number of scholars like Cantillon, Turgot, Hume, and Stuart etc. A reviewer expressed surprise how the mercantilist's overwhelming concern with price continued to be main subject matter with Smith, who was aware of the importance of the dynamic changes in productive techniques and industrial organization within the business enterprise in the era of English industrial revolution. While first commentator argued that Adam Smith's concept of competition mainly related to price mechanism alone, the second pointed out that Adam Smith's vision of competition goes beyond price determination within markets. In order to support his viewpoint, he quoted from Wealth of Nations referring to means like new division of labor, new improvements in art, which would have been never thought of in absence of competition among producers. However, the later reviewer apparently agreed with the former when he argues that Adam Smith and other classical economist's related competition more to the issues of resource allocation and theory of value than to productive efficiency.

Richardson (1975) argues that the concept of competition in the Wealth of Nations relates to two distinct phenomena.

The first meaning related to balancing of supply and demand in particular markets. ·Evolution of structural and technological forces is the second interpretation. Smith offers a theory of economic equilibrium on the one hand and a theory of economic evolution on the other in Wealth of Nations. Competition has a role to play in both of them. Let us elaborate.

Smith describes how actual prices tend to gravitate to their natural or cost determined level. Competition is shown to be necessary to the process. It is pointed out monopoly by raising prices and reducing supply would "derange more or less the natural distribution of the stock of money". Smith identifies the tendency towards equilibrium and implies the resulting allocation of resources is optimal from society's point of view.

In his theory of economic evolution, Smith has advanced a disequilibrium theory in which he views the economy as in a state of constant and internally generated change. Perpetual motion results from the fact that division of labor is both a cause and effect of economic progress. Smith discusses how division of labor increases wealth on the one hand and widens market on the other. Widening of the market would lead to increased wealth, which in turn would lead division of labor be carried forward. The dynamic character of the interaction may not be fully appreciated till one recognizes the extent of market also depends on wealth, which in turn is created by division of labor (Young, 1928). Thus in the Wealth of Nations, competition apart from equating demands and supplies within the context of a given industrial structure and a given technology, has also to adapt both structure and technology to the fresh opportunities created by expanding markets. While there are two distinct interpretations of competition in Wealth of nations, problems arose later. It is because of the fact theorists succeeding Smith (except Marshall) attended things that could be easily handled. They focused on that interpretation of competition, which is easier between the two. The equilibrating and allocative functions of competition are discussed exclusively reducing technical progress to an exogenous variable and ignoring structural evolution. Later writers, concerned with more analytical rigor, developed the theory of equilibrium in a way, which is clearly very different from that implicit in Smith's theory of evolution. Existence of Smith's theory of economic evolution went unnoticed, and so the notion of competition contained therein.

While the classical economists viewed competition as a market process, the emergence of the concept of competition as a market structure is a distinctive contribution of the neoclassical economics. The groundwork for this development was laid by Cournot followed by attempts by Jevons and Edgeworth at marrying the concepts of competition and market. Such an attempt finally led to the current concept of perfect competition, after refinements by Clark and Knight. Stigler viewed this marriage as unfortunate as each deserved a separate treatment. Interestingly, the concept of competition has been accorded a subsidiary status to the concept of market. Hayek argues that the theory of perfect competition has little claim to be called competition.

He stresses that perfect knowledge and foresight would create a paralyzing influencing effect on all action. It is not possible to argue that perfect competition is a model of competition because it is only through competition that knowledge will be discovered. The real basis for comparison with existing competition is not perfect competition; Perfect competition would exist if competition in the Smithian sense were prevented from operating.

The classical view regards competition as the antithesis of monopoly. Thus competition was viewed as absence of monopoly power is. It was left to Chamberlain to reconcile economic theory with the fact that it is not possible for a firm to compete without monopolizing and hence much of the business world is a mixture of competition and monopoly. Every act of competition on the part of a businessman is evidence of some degree of monopoly power in economic theory.

Thus while he recognized that most markets are to some extent both controlled and controlling, it has limited relevance as a guide in implementing policies in order to be meaningful for economic policy seeking to restrain monopoly and promote competition. While the traditional distinction between competition and monopoly is a non-starter, the merging of these two concepts in a theory of monopolistic competition avoided defining a concept of competition.

Chamberlin's concept of monopolistic competition as a market structure characterised by large numbers with free entry and product differentiation but without recognition of interdependence is now regarded as being only trivially different from perfect competition and may be as rare as perfect competition. Product differentiation takes place typically in a market environment of competition among the few. Chamberlin's contribution in section 4 of chapter 3 of his book relating to "mutual dependence recognized" is not a core part of his contribution and constitutes original contribution to theory of oligopoly.

The root of the ambiguity of the meaning of the term competition is attributed to the failure to distinguish between the idea of competition and the idea of market structure. The common feature of perfect competition and monopoly is that both rule out the possibility of any competitive behavior. In monopoly, there is no one to compete. Perfect competition, ironically is a state of passive adjustment. Neither is there any competition through quality, because products are homogenous, nor is there any price competition because there can be no price-cutting. Also there can be no non-price competition, because there is no product differentiation. So the only form of competition can be cost reducing competition. What is insufficiently emphasized is that perfect competition is a state of affairs totally incompatible with the idea of any and all competition. All other forms of competition except perfect competition are an admixture of monopoly and competition.

Both perfect competition and monopoly mean absence of competition but reasons are distinct in each case. Monopoly is a market situation in which intraindustry competition has been done away with by means of identifying the firm as the industry. Perfect competition, on the other hand is a market situation, which as a result of free entry of a large number of formerly competing firms has evolved to the point of equilibrium where no further competition within the industry is possible. Schumpeter's notion of competition views of competition sees it less as a process for allocating given stock of resources and reduction in prices for an existing set of products and in the form of new and improved ideas, new products, new production processes, new marketing techniques, new organizational structures etc. Such competition strikes at the foundations of the life of the existing firms and not merely at their outputs and profits. Twentieth century competition apparently resembles Schumpeter's notion of competition as price competition between firms has given way to competition on the basis of product improvements and cost advantages generated by developments in methods of production and organization. In this view, innovation is the major mechanism by which firms compete. According to Schumpeter, there are three stages in the process of change.

The first stage is invention: It relates to the generation of a new idea and its subsequent development to a point where the conceptual and practical difficulties of its implementation have been overcome.

The second stage is innovation, which occurs when entrepreneur believes that it is worthwhile to commercialize the invention. He distinguishes among five types of innovations. There is a tendency to narrowly focus on introduction of new products, and processes, which incorporate technological change. His broader definition of innovation covers more of the ways in which use of resource may be improved. This includes improvement in the quality of existing products, development of a new market, exploitation of new source of supply and adoption of improved organizational routines.

The entrepreneur cannot know in advance whether his innovation will succeed or not. If expectations are correct, then the innovation generates abnormal profits, as a result of either increasing revenue or reducing costs and leads to creation of temporary monopolistic advantages over competitors. But successful innovation creating transitory monopolies create pockets of profits which in turn provide the incentive for the imitators to step forward and thereby drive these profits to zero. This is Schumpeter's third stage: diffusion. As a result of widespread imitation, the innovation becomes established as the basis for future invention and innovation. Schumpeter's notion of competition is a process of creative destruction. Innovation creating monopoly, monopoly creating profits, profits creating imitators until a state of normalcy returns only to be followed by new innovations and repeat of a cycle. Thus, whereas the first view sees monopoly as antithesis of competition, the second views monopoly as an integral part of dynamically competitive process and a passing stage in industry's evolution. Competition displaces existing products and methods of production by new ones. Hence from day to day there are winners and losers. This representation of competitive process owes its origin to Joseph Schumpeter.

Schumpeter's notion of competition views of competition sees it less as a process for allocating given stock of resources and reduction in prices for an existing set of products and in the form of new and improved ideas, new products, new production processes, new marketing techniques, new organizational structures etc. Such competition strikes at the foundations of the life of the existing firms and not merely at their outputs and profits. Twentieth century competition apparently resembles Schumpeter's notion of competition as price competition between firms has given way to competition on the basis of product improvements and cost advantages generated by developments in methods of production and organization. In this view, innovation is the major mechanism by which firms compete. According to Schumpeter, there are three stages in the process of change. The first stage is invention: It relates to the generation of a new idea and its subsequent development to a point where the conceptual and practical difficulties of its implementation have been overcome.

The second stage is innovation, which occurs when entrepreneur believes that it is worthwhile to commercialize the invention. He distinguishes among five types of innovations. There is a tendency to narrowly focus on introduction of new products, and processes, which incorporate technological change. His broader definition of innovation covers more of the ways in which use of resource may be improved. This includes improvement in the quality of existing products, development of a new market, exploitation of new source of supply and adoption of improved organizational routines.

The entrepreneur cannot know in advance whether his innovation will succeed or not. If expectations are correct, then the innovation generates abnormal profits, as a result of either increasing revenue or reducing costs and leads to creation of temporary monopolistic advantages over competitors. But successful innovation creating transitory monopolies create pockets of profits which in turn provide the incentive for the imitators to step forward and thereby drive these profits to zero. This is Schumpeter's third stage: diffusion. As a result of widespread imitation, the innovation becomes established as the basis for future invention and innovation. Schumpeter's notion of competition is a process of creative destruction.

Innovation creating monopoly, monopoly creating profits, profits creating imitators until a state of normalcy returns only to be followed by new innovations and repeat of a cycle. Thus, whereas the first view sees monopoly as antithesis of competition, the second views monopoly as an integral part of dynamically competitive process and a passing stage in industry's evolution. Competition displaces existing products and methods of production by new ones. Hence from day to day there are winners and losers. This representation of competitive process owes its origin to Joseph Schumpeter.

The ideas of the Austrian school originate in Karl Menger and proponents include Mises and Hayek. Economic freedom is the hallmark of competition and is deemed to be limited only in so far as the rights of other people are not infringed. Hayek argued that individual freedom gives rise to spontaneous order which as not been deliberately designed by any one. The spontaneity of individual behavior gives rise to an open ended process the outcome of which can not predicted. While economic freedom is the best suited for safeguarding the individual welfare, welfare maximum cannot be identified in advance. As opposed to a static market structure of perfect competition, Austrians see of competition as a process of discovery by which economic agents seek to enhance their welfare and thus attempt to reach an optimum over time in an uncertain and changing world. Most efficient techniques and products appealing most to the consumers cannot be anticipated with certainty without putting unknown and untried techniques and novel products to the test of the market. The price of a successful product commands may exceed average costs. Success is thus rewarded by profitability, which in turn provides incentives for further innovations. A deficient state of knowledge is thus overcome by competition as a process of discovery.

Within the new institutional economics, the Austrian and evolutionary approaches have more in common with each other than with neoclassical economics. In both approaches competition is characterized by uncertainty and flux. Experiments must be conducted by firms to identify, which actions lead to improved performance and must judge for example, whether to imitate the other firms or innovate in more fundamental ways. Uncertainty thus prevails not only with the strategy of the firms but also the result of adoption of any particular strategy.

A significant difference prevails between these two notions of competitive process. In Austrian economics, whatever the firm's financial performance, the entrepreneur actively seeks improvement. In the evolutionary approach, firms are less aware and less proactive. If the firm's current performance is acceptable (that is if covers the opportunity cost of the resources deployed) no change will be initiated. They react to the environment and seek improvement only when survival is threatened. Truly speaking, the Austrian notion of the world is more desirable where the firms always seek improvement despite their financial performance and thus competition in Austrian notion of competition is also a self-propelled process, which is not quite consistent with observations. In Austrian world there is no X-inefficiency. A definition of competition has been provided by Stigler (1987) Competition is rivalry between two individuals (or groups or nations) and it arises whenever two or more parties strive for something that all cannot obtain. Vickers (1995) points out the following characteristics of this definition.

- The breadth of the definition encompasses all forms, instruments and objects of rivalry.
- It is a behavioural definition of competition as opposed to the analytical concept of perfect competition.
- Identification of competition with rivalry does not mean more competition is an end in itself.

4

EQUILIBRIUM CONDITION AND AGGREGATE CREDIT

INTRODUCTION

The real side of our model should now be fairly clear. The adverse shocks in our model are merely delays in the timing of production - adverse shocks to total production would only exacerbate the problems. Even though the total production possibilities of the economy over dates 2 and 4 do not change with increases in late projects, the amount of consumption goods available at date 2 (aggregate real liquidity) falls. Given an excess of demand over supply for liquidity, the real interest rate will rise, increasing supply as banks restructure more late projects, until the market clears. The number of projects funded to maturity falls. We will expand on this shortly. Since initial investors can express their purchasing power only with their claims on the bank, the demand for consumption at date 2 is their (real) deposit claim on the bank. Thus market clearing implies the demand for real liquidity (that is, for date-2 goods) is less than the supply, so 2 d Goods available for consumption on or before date-2 (2.3) where we will derive a specific expression for the right hand side shortly.

Because demand deposits are real and investors are unwilling to substitute future consumption, goods prices at date 2 will not affect demand. Since all initial goods are invested in the bank, which further invests in projects, the supply of date-2 real consumption goods can only come from early projects or from restructured late projects. More supply can only come from more restructuring, so the only price that can adjust to clear the market is the real interest rate, r24, which determines bank's incentives to restructure late projects.

NOMINAL DEPOSITS AS A HEDGE AGAINST AGGREGATE LIQUIDITY SHORTAGES

Instead of real deposits, let banks have nominal deposits outstanding at date 0, which let the depositor withdraw 0 units of cash on demand. Deposits will return the nominal rate, i02, if rolled over until date 2, so they will pay 2 0 *i02.

If the fiscal demand determines the value of money, the bank issues nominal deposits, and there is some such that the representative bank survives, then the representative bank will not fail no matter what the actual realization of.

We do require some conditions: First, each bank's loan portfolio has to be representative of aggregate economic activity, that is, bank portfolios should be similar.

If not, then banks with low i can fail, even when they have issued nominal deposits. Of course, given our results that prices adjust to aggregate liquidity, there exists a set of cross-subsidies from high banks to low banks that will keep all the banks alive. These cross-subsidies may not be privately rational for a healthy bank but may be in the collective interest.

Second, for the fiscal demand to provide a value of nominal claims that is proportional to the discounted value of real production, taxation should also be proportional to aggregate production (for example, a linear sales tax).

Discussion

When a bank offers nominal deposit contracts, its real repayment burden depends on the value of moving into cash at each instant. We have modeled one reason this value could rise -- too little money in the system can depress the price of cash goods and make cash transactions extremely lucrative - but there are others.

Nominal deposits make the bank highly susceptible to fleeting opportunities available in the cash market (or, equivalently, other exogenous changes in the money demand function). This indicates the desirability of policies to offset temporary shocks to money demand that are unrelated to total output.

Important prior work has noted un-accommodated shocks to money demand can cause "panics" when banks issue nominal liabilities (see Champ, Smith and Williamson [1996]).

There are two particularly important differences in our paper. First, the demand for money in Champ et al. [1996] comes from easily identified "movers" who demand it inelastically to carry it as a store of value to another location. This implies that if there are too many movers, relative price changes cannot deter them from withdrawing currency, and the constant quantity of currency is shared pro-rata among movers.

The reduced value obtained by those who withdraw implies that depositors who do not move do not want to withdraw, and do not have to be paid to stay in. By contrast, in our model, all depositors face the outside opportunity that causes them to want to withdraw. Given that demand for currency is elastic, the potential currency drain, or more generally, potential conversions of deposits to other uses (or even currencies), raises the rate that the bank has to pay. Even if the actual currency "drain" is small, bank health can be impaired.

The second difference follows from the first: a panic in their model is simply a loss of reserves from banks. No banks actually fail as a result of high demand for cash because withdrawers are rationed pro-rata.

The critical feature in our model, by contrast, is that a high transaction demand for cash translates into a higher payout on all deposits, which can affect aggregate credit, and in extremis, impair the solvency of the bank. Thus not only will there be a premium on cash during panics, but also banks will fail, as the historic evidence indeed suggests.

CRISES OF BANKING THEORY

In order to protect the public's confidence in deposit money, governments usually guarantee bank deposits implicitly or through an explicit deposit insurance system.

Thus bank insolvency does not induce immediate bank runs.

In many episodes of banking crises, several years passed quietly after bank insolvency had occurred, with the insolvency continuing to develop under the surface, and the rash of bank failures broke out only when the bank insolvency exceeded a certain level.

In this chapter I present a simple model that describes the dynamics of bank insolvency in a form that eventually results in banking system failure or bank recapitalization by the government. The main results are as follows:

(1) The government cannot indefinitely postpone recognizing the fiscal loss associated with bank insolvency.

(2) The consumption level is too high (low) before (after) bank recapitalization compared with the optimal level. Thus the price conditions become deflationary (inflationary) before (after) bank recapitalization.

(3) Social welfare decreases as bank recapitalization is delayed.

In the recent episodes of banking crises, the crises have developed through the following dynamics (Caprio and Klingebiel [1997]).

First of all bank insolvency develops as a result of a collapse of an asset-price bubble or increase in inefficient lending. Even though insolvency becomes severe, bank failures are prevented for several years by deposit guarantees from the government or liquidity support from the central bank.

Under the surface, though, the bank insolvency continues to swell as time passes, and a system-wide rash of bank failures breaks out at the point when the bank insolvency becomes apparent to the general public or market participants.

This pattern of crisis development is consistent with many episodes of banking crises, such as in the United States (1980s) and Japan (1990s).

One major factor that produces this dynamic, it seems to me, is the special role of bank deposits.

In modern economies, bank deposits play an important role as a means of payment. On the one hand, they are private liabilities of banks, and on the other hand, they are public goods: deposit money.

In order to protect the public's confidence in deposit money, governments usually guarantee bank deposits implicitly or through an explicit deposit insurance system. If bank deposits were unprotected private liabilities just like ordinary corporate debts, the occurrence of bank insolvency would trigger bank runs immediately, and the losses associated with bank insolvency would be recognized and borne by the depositors immediately.

Since, however, the government guarantees bank deposits and the central bank provides liquidity to support the banking system, bank runs do not necessarily happen when banks become insolvent. As a result, even after bank insolvency occurs, deposit money backed by no bank assets can continue to circulate for a considerable period of time.

Unbacked deposit money is an implicit liability of the government. If the government decides that it is unwilling to let depositors bear the losses resulting from bank insolvency, it has no other choice than to make up for the losses itself, ultimately meaning the use of taxpayers' money.

In what follows, I use the term bank recapitalization to refer to this form of banking system recapitalization through the injection of taxpayers' money. To inject taxpayer's money into the banking system is an unpopular policy and politically difficult to implement.

The government usually tries to put off recognizing bank insolvency and making up for the losses. Therefore, the government is tempted to continue an unsustainable policy: on the one hand, it declares deposit guarantees and provides liquidity support, and on the other hand, it postpones bank recapitalization.

The model in this paper describes the development of bank insolvency and the response of macroeconomic variables under this unsustainable policy. There is a literature in which the response of an economy to an unsustainable policy is theoretically examined, namely, the research on balance of payment crises (Krugman [1979], Calvo [1987]).

In the models of BOP crises, a policy of fixing the exchange rate at unsustainable level causes the crisis.

The intuition of my model is similar. In my model, the unsustainable policy (deposit guarantees without bank recapitalization) causes an inefficient outcome.2 The paper which is closest to this paper is Dekle and Kletzer (2003). While I developed this model independently, the structure of my model is qualitatively very close to theirs, with some differences in the policy lessons: They stress that the stringent supervision that requires loan-loss reserving by banks is important to prevent the banking crisis, while I argue that quick recapitalization of banks are necessary once the banking system falls into insolvency as a result of an exogenous shock.

There are some empirical findings on banking crises that are consistent with this model:

(1) Output losses following a banking crisis are observed for a surprisingly long period of time (Boyd, Kwak, and Smith [2002]).

(2) In a country that experienced a single crisis, the inflation rate typically falls after the onset of the bank insolvency (Boyd et al. [2001]).

(3) Open-ended liquidity support and unlimited deposit guarantees are significant contributors to the fiscal cost of a banking crisis (Honohan and Klingebiel [2000]).

The organization of this paper is as follows: In the next section, I present the basic structure of the model.

REMARKS

If banks can default on their deposit liabilities when their assets are impaired as a result of an asset-price bubble collapse or some other macroeconomic shock, the optimal allocation (ct, kt) = (co, ko) can be realized in a competitive equilibrium. But since bank deposits circulate in the economy as money, the government generally does not allow the occurrence of defaults on bank deposits, and people generally expect that it will not.

The government will guarantee the deposits and provide liquidity to banks with the result that bank deposits in excess of bank assets continue circulating in the economy. The government has no other choice than to make up for the gap between liabilities and assets of banks at some point by using taxpayer's money in order to restore the solvency of the banking system.

But since bank recapitalization policy is politically unpopular, the government tries to delay recapitalization. This paper examined the consequences of this unsustainable policy, namely, deposit guarantees (and liquidity support) without recapitalization of the banking sector.

One of our main findings is that the government cannot postpone bank recapitalization forever.

The degree of the impairment of bank assets and other technological constraints determine the time limit for postponement.

If the time limit comes without recapitalization, the banking system will collapse, and the government will be forced to make up for the losses from bank insolvency by using taxpayers' money. Social welfare decreases as bank recapitalization is delayed.

The consumption level before (after) recapitalization is too high (low) compared with the optimal level. Thus the price conditions before (after) recapitalization become deflationary (inflationary). The reason that the outcome becomes inefficient is the distortion in financing the cost of bank recapitalization:

Consumers anticipating a tax increase after recapitalization set their level of consumption too high for the period before recapitalization.

This inefficiency can be avoided if the government allows the occurrence of defaults on bank deposits, i.e., bank recapitalization through a lump-sum transfer from consumers. But this is not an option for a government that wants to maintain the public's confidence in deposit money. Thus, in the situation where the government cannot use a lump-sum transfer to finance bank recapitalization, bank insolvency causes distortions of resource allocation in any case.

There may be another source of distortion associated with bank insolvency that is not modeled in this paper. It is uncertain how the cost of making up for the gap between bank liabilities and assets will be financed in a real-life banking crisis. The government may finance the cost by, for example, inflation, or increases in labor taxes or capital taxes.

This uncertainty about cost distribution can be an additional source of inefficiency in the model where consumers are risk averse. There seem to exist several mechanisms by which the circulation of deposit money on which banks cannot easily default causes a serious distortion in a case of bank insolvency; this paper demonstrates one such mechanism.

MONETARY POLICY AND ITS CHANNELS OF TRANSMISSION

Thus far, we have examined what happens when the quantities of money and bonds are fixed, and endogenous price level adjustments cause the real value of nominal deposits to vary.

If, however, the endogenous adjustments do not serve to stabilize the system, monetary policy, by changing the quantities of money and bonds, can influence the price levels and, thereby, the real obligations of banks, and thus cause a better match between the aggregate liquidity demand and supply. Monetary policy could be thought of as part of the optimal contract, if there was a way to commit to replicate the optimal state-contingent policy. In particular, policies that prevent inefficient bank failures can be desireable.

Effects of Policy Changes

Given real parameters B and G , bank solvency, liquidity, and credit decisions will be determined by the required real repayment on deposits at date 2. Both the date 0 price level (for cash goods), P02, and the date 1 price level, P12, are critical here.

If P02 is very low relative to P12 because of a shortage of money relative to cash goods, the real quantity depositors can get by withdrawing at date 0 goes up.

In order to prevent all depositors from withdrawing, the bank will have to pay depositors a nominal interest rate that equalizes the real goods they can purchase by withdrawing at date 0 and the real goods they can purchase by writing checks at date 1 (since the gross real rate is 1 between these dates, they will then be indifferent between the two choices).

But this means that when cash is at a premium, the date-0 price of cash goods determines the required date-2 real payout of the bank.

The way to reduce the real obligations of the bank is then to raise the date-0 price by increasing the supply of money, M0. Open market operations that exchange money for bonds at date 0 will be effective in this case and lead to lower future real rates, greater credit, and more solvent banks.

Of course, once there is enough money supply such that net nominal interest rates are driven to zero (P02 = P12), open market operations are no longer effective because the price level P02 is determined by the sum of money and bonds and not by money alone.

Put another way, money no longer has a liquidity premium because cash goods are no longer cheaper than produced goods, the nominal interest rate is zero, and money and bonds are equivalent so exchanging one for the other has no effect.

Even so, the government can still affect credit by printing more money or bonds and transferring them to agents (a "helicopter drop") to inflate prices (alternatively, one could think about a credible reduction in the tax rate), thus reducing the real liabilities of the banking system. We examine the mechanics of all this in what follows.

The Liquidity Channel of Transmission of Monetary Policy

To see the channel working, consider an open market repurchase conducted by the monetary authority, which has the effect of increasing the date-0 money supply to 0 M and reducing the face value of outstanding date-2 bonds to 2 02 B i where is a small number.

To focus on the pure effect of the open market operation, let no other exogenous parameter be changed at this or other dates. The open market repurchase takes place after initial contracts are negotiated and projects initiated, and is executed so that banks have the added money at date 0.

If both types of banks survive without intervention, then so long as the gross nominal interest rate exceeds 1 and some late projects are being restructured, an open market repurchase of bonds with money at date 0 reduces the nominal interest rate, increases total credit and reduces the fraction of late projects restructured.

Corollary 1:

(i) Open market operations may be effective but no longer feasible if the outstanding stock of bonds is fully bought back and the gross nominal interest rates still exceeds one.

(ii) Further open market operations are ineffective if gross nominal interest rates fall to one.

(iii) In either case, if late projects are being restructured, an unrequited transfer of money or bonds from the government to agents will increase total credit and reduce the fraction of late projects restructured, with a dollar of money being more effective than a dollar of bonds when the nominal interest rate exceeds 1.

One could ask if all situations of liquidity shortage can be alleviated by nominal deposits and state contingent monetary policy, so long as the ex-ante expected return constraint of depositors is satisfied.

The answer is yes, for the price level at all dates can be driven up arbitrarily high, and the demand for liquidity made arbitrarily low simply by flooding the market with enough money and bonds.

In fact, the banking system will continue all late projects if the real value of deposits is driven below the minimum of (i) the amount of liquidity available to a B type bank when no late project is restructured and (ii) the real value of the B type bank when no late project is restructured and the real rate r24 is 1.

After this point, further monetary expansion will have no effect on real activity.

Consider again our base case example with 0.2 B 5 and nominal deposits of 0.9333. If the money supply is fixed at 0.2, the type B banks fail (implying that all type B bank projects are restructured).

A small increase in the money supply to 0.207 effected by buying down the quantity of outstanding bonds from 0.4 to 0.375 (see the proof of Corollary 1 for formulae) reduces the real value B type banks must pay out at date 2.

This allows the type B banks to be just solvent at the real interest rate that provides incentives for restructuring (r24 R 1.2), and they restructure a fraction 0.26 of their late projects but can also see all early projects to maturity.

So a small open market operation has a large effect on real activity. If the money supply at date 0 is increased to 0.234 by buying down bonds from 0.4 to 0.314, the type B banks survive without restructuring any projects (B 0) and the date-2 real interest rate 24 r falls to one.

Financial Contagion

Our simple model of money allows us to see the effects of alternative assumptions easily.

For instance, suppose depositors who run on a bank will not accept deposits on other banks but will only take money (for instance, because they need time to verify the quality of the bank they will deposit in). Bank failures can now be contagious through their effect on monetary conditions. To see this, suppose that type B banks are not expected to meet their nominal deposit obligations at date 2 and fail.

Then they will be run immediately at date 0. They will pay out their cash reserves to depositors, but once they run out, they will have to sell assets. If the only asset that their depositors will accept is cash, all bank assets must be sold for cash (and not for deposits in other banks).

These transactions will lock up cash, leaving less cash to buy cash goods. At this "fire-sale" price, the purchase of cash goods becomes even more lucrative, and forces the G type banks to pay a yet higher rate to keep their depositors from moving to cash. 13 Given the higher payout to deposits at date 2, these type G banks could also fail if their value falls below 0 P02.

This resembles the contagious bank failures described by Friedman and Schwarz (1963); Depositors run on banks, forcing banks to sell more assets for cash, which renders the money supply inadequate for the quantum of real activity, forcing a further drop in the price level, still greater incentive to withdraw, and still more bank failures.

Notes

Finally, a few notes. First, we do not need reserve requirements, capital requirements, or deposit insurance for monetary expansion to have real effects. Moreover, it is not necessary to fool the public or even surprise it. A fully anticipated pre-announced plan involving more appropriate state contingent monetary accommodation than another pre-announced plan can lead to greater credit today and credit and output in the future. As a stark example, consider a policy that prevents bank failures when only a small reduction in the real deposit burden is required; this policy will increase the ex-ante expected return on deposits, as well as credit and output.

Second, because a significant portion of bank liabilities is convertible on demand, banks are susceptible to temporary spikes in the transactions demand for money. By contrast, financial intermediaries with longer maturity liabilities are affected only if a substantial fraction of their liabilities mature together at a time of high transactions demand or shortage of liquidity supply.

A financial intermediary with longer-term liabilities that are diversified across maturities will be much less affected by fluctuations in monetary conditions, and they will be less central channels to the conduit of monetary policy.

Third, we have modeled the temporary shock as one to money demand, coming from a surge in supply of cash goods. It could equally well come from a direct increase in the demand for cash (for instancc, a flight to cash) or from temporary fluctuations in the supply of money. Finally, note there are other channels through which an exchange of money for bonds can affect the real activity of banks. In particular, it could work by altering the real value of financial assets on bank balance sheets.

In practice, it may be a less important channel for banks. More traditional effects, which require additional but traditional assumptions, can also be seen in this model. For example, because demand deposits are special -- even when uninsured -- any kind of reserve requirement on demand deposits will immediately make banks a channel of transmission (also see Stein (1998)).

Similarly, if firms have future revenues that are fixed in nominal terms, then a shortage of money can push up the nominal interest rate, reduce their net worth, and thus reduce lending (see Bernanke and Gertler (1989)).

EVIDENCE AND ROBUSTNESS

Empirical Implications

The model has four important implications:

(i) A shortage of real liquidity supply relative to real liquidity demand causes bank fragility. One obvious situation where the demand and supply of liquidity could be mismatched is when neither is under the direct control of monetary authorities and market clearing price adjustments do not insulate banks from liquidity shocks- for example, when the banking system predominantly has foreign currency deposits. One would expect, ceteris paribus, a "dollarized" banking system to be more fragile and to have greater deposit volatility than one with domestic currency deposits.

Nicolo, Honohan , and Ize (2003) find this to be the case. Banks in "dollarized" economies are, on average, more fragile: they are closer to default as measured by their Z-score or the ratio of non-performing loans to total loans. Deposit growth is also more volatile in these countries. An obvious caveat is that more fragile banking systems are more likely to issue foreign currency liabilities, and the authors use instruments to correct for this.

An example of an adverse liquidity supply shock in such countries is a cessation of external capital inflows. There is a strong correlation between such a "sudden stop" to a country, the extent of dollarization of the country's banking system, and the prevalence of banking crises (see IADB (2004)).

Finally, one example of a dramatic change in the value of money is a devaluation. In Argentina, by end 2000, an increasingly cash-strapped government with substantial debt service in dollars was tapping into the same dollar pool as the banking system, which had significant dollar liabilities of its own (see Rajan (2004) for details). As the recognition dawned that the dollar pool might not be enough at current exchange rates to service all the debt and a devaluation was likely, a domestic currency deposit run started on the banks - the current value of withdrawals (and conversion into goods or dollars) was greater than anticipated future value.

Interestingly, dollar deposits were initially more stable, though eventually the knowledge that the dollar shortage would render all banks insolvent caused a more general run.

(ii) Unaccommodated temporary increases in the demand of money will render the banking system more fragile. Mueller (1997, p326) in his history of the Venetian money market, describes how the sailing of the trading galleys was fixed for July and August. Naturally, this was a time of enormously high transactions demand for money as merchants strove to buy the goods and bullion to stock the ships. Interestingly, nominal interest rates were very high during this time, causing tremendous pressure on the banks and concentrating bank failures around this time. Soon after the galleys sailed, rates collapsed and pressure eased on the surviving banks.

(iii) A money supply which responds quickly and elastically to an increased demand for money will mitigate panics and bank failures. Champ, Smith, and Williamson (1995) examine interest rates and strains on the banking system during periods of "crop moving" in the period 1880-1910 across two systems: the United States where all U.S. currency was either a direct liability of the US government or banknotes backed by government bonds and, therefore, relatively inelastic, and Canada where chartered banks were free to issue notes against their general assets. The authors find the greater seasonal variation of Canadian currency (with a peak during the autumn crop moving) was associated with much smoother interest rates. Currency fluctuated less in the

United States, resulting in greater fluctuations in interest rates, peaking around the crop moving period. The banking panics of 1893 and 1907 in the United States indeed occurred during the crop moving season.

(iv) Changes in monetary policy should most affect the lending decisions of the least liquid and least creditworthy banks (low). Kashyap and Stein (2000) find that the effect of monetary policy on lending is indeed stronger for banks with less liquid balance sheets, that is, banks with lower ratios of securities to assets. Moreover, this effect is primarily due to the smallest (and thus least diversified) banks in their sample.

Other implications are less central. For instance, nominal deposits lend stability only if the monetary authority can be relied upon to be appropriately state contingent.

However, if they do not have the necessary acumen or credibility, or have conflicting goals, nominal deposits are destabilizing.

This implies that countries with histories of weak monetary management are likely to prefer real deposits (for example, through deposit dollarization) despite the attendant risks because the alternative could be worse (also see Jeanne (2003)). De Nicolo, Honohan , and Ize (2003) find that countries with weak institutions, high inflation, and high volatility of inflation "dollarize" more, but have more financial depth (M2/GDP) than similar countries that do not.

Alternative Assumptions: Sticky Prices

The pattern of response of aggregate output to monetary expansion has been well studied in the United States (see, for example, Bernanke and Gertler (1995)). One fact that is at odds with our model is that prices do not adjust rapidly.

While we think the fact that our model does not require sticky prices to obtain monetary transmission is a virtue, we need to ask how we could get transmission if prices were indeed sticky.

It turns out that a simple extension is sufficient. Consider a very simple search model where dealers first post prices at the beginning of the period and buyers search for a seller. If the price cannot vary with supply or demand changes, goods must be rationed. Assume the probability of a buyer meeting a dealer is an increasing function of the ratio of supply of cash goods to demand at the posted price, P02.

The nominal supply of goods at date 0 is q1P02 and the nominal demand is the total amount of cash withdrawn at date 0 by depositors.

An open market operation that increases the amount of cash that can be withdrawn by depositors will decrease the probability of each withdrawer finding a dealer. As this probability decreases, the return from withdrawing cash falls toward the return of holding cash to buy goods one period later, and the nominal interest rate on bank deposits between dates 0 and 1 will fall.

The real payout burden on deposits at date 2 falls with an expansionary open market operation, much as in the case of flexible prices. While sticky prices prevent the real price level from changing immediately with changes in monetary policy, an immediate increase in the supply of money will reduce the real value of withdrawing to make an immediate purchase.

Alternative Assumptions: Nominal Loans

We have discussed real loans thus far, with nominal or real deposits. This is consistent with the assumption that resources are in short supply so the borrowing entrepreneur promises to pay out the maximum possible ex ante by agreeing to an extremely high nominal repayment on demand. As a result, actual repayments on project loans are renegotiated down to the underlying real collateral value of assets. By contrast, bank deposits are enforced through the threat of collective action, so their nominal face value matters, regardless of how high it is. It is, however, interesting to discuss whether the system stabilizes automatically through the price level if the nominal repayment on the project loan, L, were set at a level that did not exceed the collateral value of underlying project assets (e.g., L CPjk).

If the fiscal demand for money dominates and project loans are always nominal, then:

(a) If deposits are also nominal, the representative bank will never fail at any if it is solvent and liquid at some'.

(b) If deposits are real, the representative bank becomes (weakly) less solvent as falls. Even if it is solvent at an ', it can fail at some < '.

When financial assets are all nominal and effectively have the same maturity, changes in the price level have no effect on a bank's nominal solvency, and cannot push a bank from solvency to insolvency (or vice versa). However, price level changes will change the real value of deposits and influence the real excess demand for liquidity. So long as there is a binding liquidity constraint, policy induced increases in the price level will reduce the excess liquidity demand, and will increase aggregate credit. When loans are nominal but deposits are real, an increase in the price level reduces the value of the bank's assets without affecting liabilities. Since, ceteris paribus, a fall in the economy wide fraction of early projects, (weakly) increases the price level, it can impair solvency. Automatic changes in the price level do not stabilize the banking system when it has this kind of asset-liability mismatch.

Alternative assumption: Capital

For simplicity, banks in our model do not issue capital. Clearly, capital can buffer some of the effects of liquidity shortages but it will also reduce the ability of the bank to commit to pay depositors.

An optimal capital structure will typically have the bank issuing a significant proportion of its capital structure in deposits (see Diamond and Rajan (2000)) and, as we show in the working paper version of this paper, liquidity shortages still are possible and all our results continue to hold. The issuance of capital (or heterogeneity in project returns) will, however, result in a much smoother and plausible path of real interest rates, 24 r.

MONEY AND BANKING

We now introduce a role for money. Not only will this help us flesh out the date-2 real value of financial assets in (2.2) and the right hand side of (2.3), it will also let us determine the real value of nominal deposits and show when they can serve as a hedge. We focus on two natural sources of value for money. First, money can serve as a store of value; we introduce this into our finite horizon economy by assuming that money (and any maturing government liability) can be used to pay future taxes. This generates a demand for nominal claims which we shall call the fiscal demand. Second, currency facilitates certain transactions that by their very nature are unexpected, opportunistic, small-volume, or worth concealing so that the use of formal credit is ruled out. This is the transactions demand for money. Both demands will be important in understanding the link between money and banking.

Transactions Demand

Start first with the transactions demand. Dealers, whom we referred to earlier but did not describe, receive an endowment of a perishable good, which can be sold only for cash (to fix ideas, the good is their labor, and they do not report income to the tax authorities so they accept only cash). "Early" dealers obtain an endowment 1 q of this cash good at date 1 while "late" dealers obtain 3 q at date 3 (recall that all quantities are per unit of initial project financed). One unit of this cash good is a perfect substitute for one unit of the production good. Unlike the cash good, both deposits and cash can be used to pay for the production good.

To introduce a motive for trade, we assume that no one can consume his own endowment or production. All trades require payment one period ahead in cash or deposits. This means that in order to consume a cash good that is produced at date j, the buyer has to pay cash to the seller at date j-1. If he wants to consume a production good, he also has the option of writing a check to the seller at date j-1, which will clear against the funds he has on deposit at date j. The seller can use the cash or deposit he receives at date j to buy goods for consumption at date j+1. This payment in advance constraint also applies to sales of bonds (to be described) and restructured loans. Finally, if a bank issues deposits (in exchange for cash, bonds or loans) at date j, they can be used to initiate transactions at date j.

Let Pjk denote the price in date j cash of a unit of date k consumption. For example, a transaction for date 4 goods initiated at date 3 in cash at price P34 yields the seller P34 units of cash at date 4.

The Fiscal Demand

The government taxes sales of produced goods at the rate t . To maintain consistency with the expressions derived thus far, assume that the production quantities specified earlier are aftertax, so total nominal taxes due on a project that matures at date j are 1 tC t Pj 1, j . Because cash goods may lie outside the formal economy, we assume they are not taxed -- nothing significant depends on this. Taxes are due at the time of production and are payable in cash or through a check on a deposit (with the bank then transferring the cash to the government).

The odd-numbered dates, 1 and 3, simply make payment and settlement explicit. Since date 3 is close to date 4, we allow actions at date 4 to be committed to at date 3, so late entrepreneurs can borrow deposits at date 3 against what they will have at date 4 after repaying the bank loan (= (1)C P34). They can use the resulting deposits at date 3 to purchase goods for consumption at date 4. Similarly, the banker can also issue himself deposits at date 3 against his date-4 rents. This saves us the need to introduce another date to clear purchases initiated at date 4.

Bank Failures

If the liquidity shortage is severe enough, there are two reasons banks with real deposits can fail. First, there can be insufficient aggregate output to allow all deposits to be repaid even if all late loans are called and projects restructured. Second, it is possible that type B banks are insolvent at the real interest rate that must prevail for banks to have incentives to call in loans at a loss and force projects to be restructured.

Recall that if a bank is expected to fail, depositors run and demand payment immediately on the revelation of uncertainty at date 0. Since projects pay at date 2 at the earliest, and since the bank obtains more from restructuring rather than selling the illiquid project loans to satisfy depositor demands at date 0, all projects of a failing bank are restructured, including the early ones that would pay off at date 2.

Failure is inefficient because early projects could have produced C in a timely manner to satisfy early consumption needs, but now produce only c.

The specificity of bank relationships means that bank failures can cause a persistent drop in real activity, as in Bernanke [1983]. The collective action problem inherent in demand deposits is now destructive for it forces the costly production of consumption goods at a time when they are not really needed. When bank contracts are real, the real interest rate, r24, is the only price which can adjust to clear markets. The system may have insufficient degrees of freedom to adjust to an adverse shock without the stark consequences we have documented-major changes in credit and possibly bank failures.

This real model is not without practical interest - when a country's banking system has deposits denominated in foreign exchange (or if the country were on the Gold standard), it is as if the banks issue real deposits. But our primary purpose is to make clear that credit contraction and failure are essentially real phenomena and occur when the bank is squeezed between non-renegotiable demand deposits and a limited production of consumption goods.

If fully state-contingent deposit contracts were available, where the real face value of each deposit depended on the individual bank's situation and the aggregate state of nature, then the banking system would produce a given amount of liquidity (expected date 2 consumption) at the minimum cost of foregone future (date 4) consumption.

The outcomes with such contracts are easily characterized.

First, early projects should never be restructured because it increases the cost of providing liquidity with no offsetting benefit. A necessary and sufficient condition for avoiding restructuring of early projects is that there be no runs.

Second, the minimum number of late projects should be restructured, in order to just meet the consumption needs of investors; none should be restructured if goods are to be stored, or consumed by those who are willing to consume late. This condition will also be met if there are no runs. Last, in order to minimize the date 4 cost of a given amount of expected date 2 consumption, if late projects must be restructured in some states of nature, then the contingent deposit payment in all other states should at least be all of the return from the early projects.

Explicit and full state contingency may not be possible for the usual technological and institutional reasons. The real interest rate, with just two values in our model, offers limited additional contingency even if observable and verifiable. However, deposits could be made implicitly contingent by denominating them in cash, so that their real value can fluctuate with the price level.

If the price level rises with production delays, the real payout on deposits will fall, reducing liquidity demand. Nominal deposits will thus offer a hedge against the consequences of aggregate shortages. Because banks are of heterogeneous types ex-post, automatic movements in the state contingent value of money cannot possibly replicate complete state contingent contracts, but they can be "contingent enough" to hedge the banking system as a whole against runs. In what follows, we describe conditions under which nominal deposits can hedge the banking system as a whole against real shocks. But we go on to show that it also exposes the system to monetary shocks.

5

INVENTION OF THE BANKING AND COINAGE

INTRODUCTION

Eventually private houses in Mesopotamia also got involved in these banking operations and laws regulating them were included in the code of Hammurabi. The invention of banking preceded that of coinage. Banking originated in Ancient Mesopotamia where the royal palaces and temples provided secure places for the safe-keeping of grain and other commodities. Receipts came to be used for transfers not only to the original depositors but also to third parties. In Egypt too the centralization of harvests in state warehouses also led to the development of a system of banking.

Written orders for the withdrawal of separate lots of grain by owners whose crops had been deposited there for safety and convenience, or which had been compulsorily deposited to the credit of the king, soon became used as a more general method of payment of debts to other persons including tax gatherers, priests and traders. Even after the introduction of coinage these Egyptian grain banks served to reduce the need for precious metals which tended to be reserved for foreign purchases, particularly in connection with military activities. Precious metals, in weighed quantities, were a common form of money in ancient times. The transition to quantities that could be counted rather than weighed came gradually. On page 29 of A History of Money Glyn Davies points out that the words "spend", "expenditure", and "pound" (as in the main British monetary unit) all come from the Latin "expendere" meaning "to weigh". On page 74 the author points out that the basic unit of weight in the Greek speaking world was the "drachma" or "handful" of grain, but the precise weight taken to represent this varied considerably, for example from less than 3 grams in Corinth to more than 6 grams in Aegina. Throughout much of the ancient world the basic unit of money was the stater, meaning literally "balancer" or "weigher". The talent is a monetary unit with which we are familiar with from the Parable of the Talents in the Bible. The talent was also a Greek unit of weight, about 60 pounds.

Many primitive forms of money were counted just like coins. Cowrie shells, obtained from some islands in the Indian Ocean, were a very widely used primitive form of money - in fact they were still in use in some parts of the world (such as Nigeria) within living memory. "So important a role did the cowrie play as money in ancient China that its pictograph was adopted in their written language for money." (page 36) Thus it is not surprising that among the earliest countable metallic money or "coins" were "cowries" made of bronze or copper, in China.

In addition to these metal "cowries" the Chinese also produced "coins" in the form of other objects that had long been accepted in their society as money e.g. spades, hoes, and knives. Although there is some dispute over exactly when these developments first took place, the Chinese tool currencies were in general use at about the same time as the earliest European coins and there have been claims that their origins may have been much earlier, possibly as early as the end of the second millennium BC.

The use of tool coins developed (presumably independently) in the West. The ancient Greeks used iron nails as coins, while Julius Caesar regarded the fact that the ancient Britons used sword blades as coins as a sign of their backwardness. (However the Britons did also mint true coins before they were conquered by the Romans).

These quasi-coins were all easy to counterfeit and, being made of base metals, of low intrinsic worth and thus not convenient for expensive purchases. True coinage developed in Asia Minor as a result of the practice of the Lydians, of stamping small round pieces of precious metals as a guarantee of their purity. Later, when their metallurgical skills improved and these pieces became more regular in form and weight the seals served as a symbol of both purity and weight. The first real coins were probably minted some time in the period 640 - 630 BC. Afterwards the use of coins spread quickly from Lydia to Ionia, mainland Greece, and Persia.

MONEY EXCHANGE AND CREDIT TRANSFER

The great variety of coinages originally in use in the Hellenic world meant that money changing was the earliest and most common form of Greek banking. Usually the money changers would carry out their business in or around temples and other public buildings, setting up their trapezium-shaped tables (which usually carried a series of lines and squares for assisting calculations), from which the Greek bankers, the trapezitai derived their name, much as our name for bank comes from the Italian banca for bench or counter. The close association between banking, money changing and temples is best known to us from the episode of Christ's overturning the tables in the Temple of Jerusalem (Matthew 21.12).

Money changing was not the only form of banking. One of the most important services was bottomry or lending to finance the carriage of freight by ships. Other business enterprises supported by the Greek bankers included mining and construction of public buildings. The most famous and richest of all was Pasion who started his banking career in 394 BC as a slave in the service of two leading Athenian bankers and rose to eclipse his masters, gaining in the process not only his freedom but also Athenian citizenship. In addition to his banking business he owned the largest shield factory in Greece and also conducted a hiring business lending domestic articles such as clothes, blankets, silver bowls etc. for a lucrative fee.

When Egypt fell under the rule of a Greek dynasty, the Ptolemies (323-30 BC) the old system of warehouse banking reached a new level of sophistication. The numerous scattered government granaries were transformed into a network of grain banks with what amounted to a central bank in Alexandria where the main accounts from all the state granary banks were recorded. This banking network functioned as a giro system in which payments were effected by transfer from one account to another without money passing. As double entry booking had not been invented credit transfers were recorded by varying the case endings of the names involved, credit entries being in the genitive or possessive case and debit entries in the dative case.

Credit transfer was also a characteristic feature of the services provided in Delos which rose to prominence in banking during the late second and third centuries BC. As a barren offshore island its inhabitants had to live off their wits and make the most of their two great assets - the island's magnificent natural harbour and the famous temple of Apollo - around which their trading and financial activities developed. Whereas in Athens banking, in its early days, had been carried on exclusively in cash, in Delos cash transactions were replaced by real credit receipts and payments made on simple instructions with accounts kept for each client.

The main commercial rivals of Delos, Carthage and Corinth, were both destroyed by Rome and consequently it was natural that the Bank of Delos should become the model most closely imitated by the banks of Rome. However their importance was limited by the Roman preference for cash transactions with coins.

Whereas the Babylonians had developed their banking to a sophisticated degree because their banks had to carry out the monetary functions of coinage (since coins had not been invented), and the Ptolemaic Egyptians segregated their limited coinage system from their state banking system to economise on the use of precious metals, the Romans preferred coins for many kinds of services which ancient (and modern) banks normally provided. After the fall of the Roman Empire banking was forgotten and had to be re-invented much later.

Banking re-emerged in Europe at about the time of the Crusades. In Italian city states such as Rome, Venice and Genoa, and in the fairs of medieval France, the need to transfer sums of money for trading purposes led to the development of financial services including bills of exchange.

Although it is possible that such bills had been used by the Arabs in the eighth century and the Jews in the tenth, the first for which definite evidence exists was a contract issued in Genoa in 1156 to enable two brothers who had borrowed 115 Genoese pounds to reimburse the bank's agents in Constantinople by paying them 460 bezants one month after their arrival.

The Crusades gave a great stimulus to banking because payments for supplies, equipment, allies, ransoms etc. required safe and speedy means of transferring vast resources of cash. Consequently the Knights of the Temple and the Hospitallers began to provide some banking services such as those already being developed in some of the Italian city states.

GREEK COINAGE

One of the smaller Greek coins was the silver obol. In the Attic standard of weights and coinage six silver obols were worth one silver drachma. It is interesting to note that before the development of coinage six of the pointed spits or elongated nails used as tool currency constituted a customary handful similar to that of the even earlier grain-based methods. Therefore one of the early Greek coins, the obol, was simply a continuation of a primitive form of money - the iron spit or pointed rod.

Inflation was a problem even in the early days of coin production. In 407 BC Sparta captured the Athenian silver mines at Laurion and released around 20,000 slaves. As a result Athens was faced with a grave shortage of coins and in 406 and 405 BC issued bronze coins with a thin plating of silver. The result was that the shortage became even worse.

Good coins tended to disappear from circulation since people naturally kept them and used the new coins instead in order to get rid of them.

This gave rise to what is probably the world's first statement of Gresham's law, that bad money drives out good, in Aristophanes' play, The Frogs, produced in 405 BC. Aristophanes wrote "the ancient coins are excellent...yet we make no use of them and prefer those bad copper pieces quite recently issued and so wretchedly struck." These base coins were demonetized in 393 BC.

Considerable rivalry developed between different currencies. "In coinage as in other matters the Greek city-states strove desperately for predominance, as did their arch-rivals the Persian emperors."

City-states with strong and widely accepted currencies would have gained prestige. In the 1960s newly independent countries in the Third World took pride in the trappings of nationhood - their own airlines, national banks, and currency. The city states of ancient Greece took a similar pride in their currencies - as is suggested by the beauty of their coins. Glyn Davies quotes another author, J. Porteous, who wrote " the fifth century saw the minting of the most beautiful coins ever made." He also quotes two historians, Austin and Vidal-Naquet, who claimed that "in the history of Greek cities coinage was always first and foremost a civic emblem. To strike coins with the badge of the city was to proclaim one's political independence."

Coercion played a role in establishing monetary uniformity. In 456 BC Athens forced Aegina to take Athenian 'owls' and to stop minting her own 'turtle' coinage and in 449 BC Athens issued an edict ordering all 'foreign' coins to be handed in to the Athenian mint and compelling all her allies to use the Attic standard of weights, measures and money. The conquests of Alexander the Great brought about a large degree of monetary uniformity over much of the known world. His father, Philip, had issued coins celebrating his triumph in the chariot race in Olympic games of 356 BC - an example of the use of coins as propaganda.

The Roman emperors made even more extensive use of coins for propaganda, one historian going so far as to claim that "the primary function of the coins is to record the messages which the emperor and his advisers desired to commend to the populations of the empire."

On pages 85-86, Glyn Davies points out that "coins were by far the best propaganda weapon available for advertising Greek, Roman or any other civilization in the days before mechanical printing was invented."

THE ROYAL MONOPOLY OF MINTING

One of the reasons for the rapid spread of the use of coins was their convenience. In situations where coins were generally acceptable at their nominal value there was no need to weigh them and in everyday transactions where relatively small numbers were involved counting was quicker and far more convenient than weighing. By the Middle Ages monarchs were able to use this convenience as a source of profit.

On page 168 Glyn Davies writes, "because of the convenience of royally authenticated coinage as a means of payment, and with hardly any other of the general means of payment available in the Middle Ages being anything like as convenient, coins commonly carried a substantial premium over the value of their metallic content, more than high enough to cover the costs of minting. Kings could turn this premium into personal profit; hence ... the wholesale regular recall of coinage... first at six yearly, then at three-yearly intervals, and eventually about every two years or so. In order to make a thorough job of this short recycling process it was essential that all existing coins should be brought in so as to maximize the profit and, in order to prevent competition from earlier issues, the new issues had to be made clearly distinguishable by the authorities yet readily acceptable to the general public."

These recoinage cycles were far more frequent than was justified by wear and tear on the coins but the profits from minting, known as seigniorage, supplemented the revenue that English monarchs raised from the efficient systems of taxation introduced by the Normans. However, revenue from minting depended on public confidence in the coinage and consequently an elaborate system of testing was introduced. "Anyone who had occasion to handle coins of silver or gold in any volume, whether merchants, traders, tax collectors, the King himself, the royal treasury, or the sheriffs, required reliable devices for testing the purity of what passed for currency." (Page 144). One of these methods was rough and ready - the use of touchstones which involved an examination of the colour trace left by the metal on the surface of a schist or quartz stone. The other, the Trial of the Pyx, was a test held in public before a jury. This Trial involved the use of 24 "touch needles", one for each of the traditional gold carats, with similar test pieces for silver.

Thus, despite the challenge of counterfeiters, governments controlled coin production and hence the money supply. Not until the rise of commercial banking and the widespread adoption of paper money was this monopoly broken, with profound consequences for the growth of democracy.

PAPER MONEY

In China the issue of paper money became common from about AD 960 onwards but there had been occasional issues long before that. A motive for one such early issue, in the reign of Emperor Hien Tsung 806-821, was a shortage of copper for making coins. A drain of currency from China, partly to buy off potential invaders from the north, led to greater reliance on paper money with the result that by 1020 the quantity issued was excessive, causing inflation. In subsequent centuries there were several episodes of hyperinflation and after about 1455, after well over 500 years of using paper money, China abandoned it.

Bills of Exchange

With the revival of banking in western Europe, stimulated by the Crusades, written instructions in the form of bills of exchange, came to be used as a means of transferring large sums of money and the Knights Templars and Hospitallers functioned as bankers. (It is possible that the Arabs may have used bills of exchange at a much earlier date, perhaps as early as the eighth century). The use of paper as currency came much later.

Goldsmith Bankers

During the English Civil War, 1642-1651, the goldsmith's safes were secure places for the deposit of jewels, bullion and coins. Instructions to goldsmiths to pay money to another customer subsequently developed into the cheque (or check in American spelling). Similarly goldsmiths' receipts were used not only for withdrawing deposits but also as evidence of ability to pay and by about 1660 these had developed into the banknote.

Virginian Tobacco

In England's American colonies a chronic shortage of official coins led to various substitutes being used as money, including, in Viriginia, tobacco, leading to the development of paper money by a different route. Tobacco leaves have drawbacks as currency and consequently certificates attesting to the quality and quantity of tobacco deposited in public warehouses came to be used as money and in 1727 were made legal tender.

Gold Standard

Although paper money obviously had no intrinsic value its acceptability originally depended on its being backed by some commodity, normally precious metals. During the Napoleonic Wars convertibility of Bank of England notes was suspended and there was some inflation which, although quite mild compared to that which has occurred in other wars, was worrying to contemporary observers who were used to stable prices and, in accordance with the recommendations of an official enquiry Britain adopted the gold standard for the pound in 1816. For centuries earlier silver had been the standard of value. The pound was originally an amount of silver weighing a pound. France and the United States were in favour of a bimetallic standard and in 1867 an international conference was held in Paris to try and widen the area of common currencies based on coins with standard weights of gold and silver. However when the various German states merged into a single country in 1871 they chose the gold standard. The Scandinavian countries adopted the gold standard shortly afterwards. France made the switch from bimetallism to gold in 1878 and Japan, which had been on a silver standard, changed in 1897. Finally, in 1900, the United States officially adopted the gold standard.

With the outbreak of the First World War in 1914 Britain decided to withdraw gold from internal circulation and other countries also broke the link with gold. Germany returned to the gold standard in 1924 when it introduced a new currency, the Reichsmark and Britain did the following year, and France in 1928. However the British government had fixed the value of sterling at an unsustainably high rate and in the worldwide economic crisis in 1931 Britain, followed by most of the Commonwealth (except Canada) Ireland, Scandinavia, Iraq, Portugal, Thailand, and some South American countries abandoned gold.

The United States kept the link to gold and after the Second World War the US dollar replaced the pound sterling as the key global currency. Other countries fixed their exchange rates against the dollar, the value of which remained defined in terms of gold. In the early 1970s the system of fixed exchange rates started to break down as a result of growing international inflation and the United States abandoned the link with gold in 1973.

Intangible Money

The break with precious metals helped to make money a more elusive entity. Another trend in the same direction is the growing interest in forms of electronic money from the 1990s onwards. In some ways e-money is a logical evolution from the wire transfers that came about with the widespread adoption of the telegraph in the 19th century but such transfers had relatively little impact on the everyday shopper.

The evolution of money has not stopped. Securitisation, the turning of illiquid assets into cash, developed in new directions in the 1990s. One much publicised development was the invention of bonds backed by intangible assets such as copyright of music, e.g.Bowie bonds, named after those issued by the popstar David Bowie. (See also Something Wild, the first novel dealing with Bowie bonds).

DEMOCRACY AND GOVERNMENT CONTROL OF THE MONEY SUPPLY

Revolutions in the form of money inevitably have political consequences. The development of modern banking and the concomitant erosion of the government's monopoly of money creation played a significant role in the development of democracy. Today, government control of the money supply faces new potential threats, the most obvious of which is the development of electronic forms of money. Another possible threat is the growth in securitisation, which has received little attention from the general public except in connection with one of its most exotic forms - Bowie bonds.

In view of these potential threats to government control of the money supply the lessons of history have great contemporary relevance.

An article in the Economist (26 November 1994 pages 25-30) entitled Electronic money: so much for the cashless society made the claim that "the transformation of the Internet from a huge virtual community into a huge virtual economy may herald the age of electronic money - and with it, headaches for traditional banks and regulators."

One of the points discussed in the Economist article was whether digital cash should be a proxy for money or whether it should be acceptable as money in its own right. The latter would, according to the article, be unpopular with governments who have always regulated banking activities carried out within their countries. "If people who log on to the Internet are localised geographically and thus subject to a particular set of national laws, the traffic that they create on the Internet is not very obviously anywhere at all." Looking further ahead the article suggests "ideally, the ultimate e-cash will be a currency without a country..."

The last time the state's monopoly over money creation was seriously weakened was when paper money was introduced and quite apart from the economic effects, that also helped to cause profound political changes as shown by the following quotations taken from the book by Glyn Davies.

Davies, Glyn. A history of money from ancient times to the present day, 3rd ed. Cardiff: University of Wales Press, 2002. 720 pages. Paperback: ISBN 0 7083 1717 0. Hardback: ISBN 0 7083 1773 1.

"Technical improvements in the media of exchange have been made for more than a millennium. Mostly they have been of a minor nature, but exceptionally there have been two major changes, the first at the end of the Middle Ages when the printing of money began to supplement the minting of coins, and the second in our own time when electronic money transfer was invented... The first stimulated the rise of banking, while the second is opening the way towards universal and instantaneous money transfer in the global village of the twenty-first century." (Page 649).

"One of the most significant but insufficiently noted results of these two major kinds of invention is the fundamental reduction they bring about in the degree of governmental monopoly power over money. When coins were the dominant form of money, monarchs were jealous of their sovereign power over their royal mints. Paper money allowed banks to become increasingly competitive sources of money, a development which led not only to significant macro-economic changes but also facilitated contemporary revolutionary constitutional changes. It was no accident that the Whigs, who supported the limited constitutional monarchy of William and Mary were prominent in promoting the Bank of England." (page 649)

"Similarly in the era of electronic banking 'national' moneys are becoming increasingly anachronistic as millions of customers, irrespective of their country of domicile, are eagerly offered a variety of competing financial institutions in a variety of competing currencies. They are spoiled for choice - and national money monopolies are thereby also being 'spoiled', in the sense of being reduced in effectiveness. The monetary authorities always try to reassert their monopolistic power - in economic jargon, to make sure that money is exogenously created - as opposed to money supplies produced elsewhere by the working of market forces - or 'endogenously' as the economists describe the process." (pages 649-650)

"The fact that more than half of the total money supply was now being created, not by the mint under the dictate of the monarch, but rather by the London money market and provincial bankers gave rise to the most profound constitutional consequences. First, in order to carry out his more burdensome civil and military duties, the monarch, after a painful but vain struggle, had been forced to call parliaments annually. Secondly because of the state's need to supplement taxes regularly and substantially with various forms of short-, medium- and long-term borrowing, the state had been forced to take into account the views and interests of the moneyed classes and the nature of the institutions which its borrowing had very largely brought into being. The national debt not only created the Bank of England but also virtually created the London money and capital markets in recognizably modern form long before an equity market in industrial shares became of importance." (page 281).

"For the first time in history money was being substantially created, not ostentatiously and visibly by the sovereign power, but mundanely by market forces..." (page 2812). Thus the constitutional reforms of the Glorious Revolution were partly caused by a financial revolution. It it is worth noting that in the following century the American Revolution was also partly the result of a dispute over paper money and the British government's control over the Colonies' money supply.

In the final chapter of the book the question of "free trade in money in a global cashless society" is considered. The economist Friedrich Hayek advocated the "de-nationalisation" of money i.e. the removal of all legal obstacles preventing individuals using whatever form of money they wanted. In that way, so he claimed, the market would produce the best forms of currency. Although Hayek was an important influence on many right wing politicians, including Margaret Thatcher, no government has been willing to go that far in giving up the state's control of money. However, the Economist article suggests that the advent of electronic cash could lead to privately issued currencies competing with official state currencies.

Another trend which some people have argued could weaken government control over currencies is securitisation, or the issuance of bonds backed by some asset. In principle almost any kind of asset could be securitised. One of the most publicised innovations in this area was the bond issue by the rock star David Bowie in 1997, using his copyrights as the security. Since then there have been quite a few similar cases in the music business. See Who's Who in Bowie Bonds for more details, or the thriller Something Wild by Linda Davies, the first novel about Bowie bonds.

Paper money was originally simply a proxy for the real thing. British banknotes still carry the phrase "I promise to pay the bearer on demand the sum of x pounds" (where "x" is the denomination of the note) with the signature of the chief cashier of the Bank of England underneath.

However, one unintended effect of the adoption of paper money was to make hyperinflation possible (e.g. the Continentals of the American Revolution, the Confederate banknotes of the US Civil War, and German notes after World War I). China which invented paper money had abandoned it, before its widespread adoption in the West, for that very reason.

In general, the more regimented and "planned" that a society is, the smaller is the role played by money. An example of this was the nations of eastern Europe and the Soviet Union before the collapse of communism. A much older, more extreme example was the Inca empire. The Incas were unique in that they managed to achieve a high degree of civilization without the use of money, though paradoxically they possessed a superabundance of what has generally been regarded as by far the best material for money - gold and silver.

Thus there is a close connection between money and liberty or, in the words of Dostoevsky, "money is coined liberty" (House of the Dead, part 1, chapter 2). Consequently, if experiments with digital cash prove successful the ramifications may ultimately extend to all forms of economic activity and have profound implications for the development of society in every country of the globe, just as the development of paper money did.

NOTEWORTHY POINTS REGARDING THE ORIGINS OF MONEY

Some of the points stressed by Glyn Davies in his book are:-

- Money did not have a single origin but developed independently in many different parts of the world.
- Many factors contributed to its development and if evidence of what anthropologists have learned about primitive money is anything to go by economic factors were not the most important.
- Money performs a variety of functions and the functions performed by the earliest types were probably fairly restricted initially and would NOT necessarily have been the same in all societies.
- Money is fungible: there is a tendency for older forms to take on new roles and for new forms to be developed which take on old roles, e.g. (this is my example) on English banknotes such as the 5 pound notes it says "I promise to pay the bearer on demand the sum of five pounds" and below that it carries the signature of the chief cashier of the Bank of England. This is a reminder that originally banknotes were regarded in Britain, and in many other countries, as a substitute for money and only later did they come to be accepted as the real thing.

Relevance of History

One of Glyn Davies's main motives for writing the book was that, as he writes in his preface around the next corner there may be lying in wait apparently quite novel problems which in all probability bear a basic similarity to those that have already been tackled with varying degrees of success or failure in other times and other places. Furthermore he is of the opinion that economists, especially monetarists, tend to overestimate the purely economic, narrow and technical functions of money and have placed insufficient emphasis on its wider social, institutional and psychological aspects.

These issues aren't simply of academic interest. Economists still argue about how to measure and control the money supply and numerous different measures, corresponding to slightly different definitions have been proposed. These disputes have implications for the material well-being of everyone, especially now that thanks to the development of computer networks, new forms of money are coming into existence. Hence the importance of learning from history.

Causes of Inflation

One of Glyn Davies's main themes is the problem of simultaneously trying to control the quality and quantity of money. He discusses many cases of inflation over the past couple of thousand years and identifies several (not necessarily mutually exclusive) causes.

Conflict between the Interests of Debtors and Creditors

The history of money is one of "unceasing conflict between the interests of debtors, who seek to enlarge the quantity of money and who seek busily to find acceptable substitutes, and the interests of creditors, who seek to maintain or increase the value of money by limiting its supply, by refusing substitutes or accepting them with great reluctance, and generally trying in all sorts of ways to safeguard the quality of money." (page 30).

The government itself is often the most important debtor and at times may be a major creditor.

> "...it is of the utmost significance to realize that because the monetary pendulum is rarely motionless at

> the point of perfect balance between the conflicting interests of creditors and debtors, so money itself is rarely 'neutral' in its effects upon the real economy and upon the fortunes of different sections of the community..." (page 32)
>
> "...the market gives no priority to posterity or the poor: silent majorities." (page 657)
>
> "In the normal course of events money is rarely 'passive' or 'neutral' while the safe haven of equilibrium on which so much economists' ink has been spilled...is equally rarely attained." (page 658)

The Fungibility of Money

"Money is so useful - in other words, it performs so many functions - that it always attracts substitutes: and the narrower its confining lines are drawn, the higher the premium there is on developing passable substitutes." (page 27).

In a discussion of the invention of money the author says: "Money has many origins - not just one - precisely because it can perform many functions in similar ways and similar functions in many ways. As an institution money is almost infinitely adaptable." (page 27).

"Money is by its very nature dynamically unstable in volume and velocity, in quantity and quality." (page 30).

Money's adaptability is chameleon-like. "Money designed for one specific function will easily take on other jobs and come up smiling. Old money very readily functions in new ways and new money in old ways: money is eminently fungible." (page 29).

One good example of fungibility is the creation of Bowie bonds. For more information see Who's Who in Bowie Bonds, or alternatively, Something Wild, a novel about Bowie bonds by Linda Davies, the daughter of Glyn Davies who is the author of A History of Money.

The Population Explosion

The author lays considerable stress on the effects of population changes on attempts to control the quality and quantity of money, pointing out that the population explosion of our times "has been a virtually silent explosion as far as monetarist literature is concerned.

Thus nowhere in Friedman's powerful, popular and influential book Free to Choose is there any mention of the population problem, nor the slightest hint that the inflation on which he is acknowledged to be the world's greatest expert might in any way be caused by the rapidly rising potential and real demands of the thousands of millions born into the world since he began his researches." (page 5).

Population pressures have had an effect on inflation in previous ages too, e.g. the so-called "Price Revolution" in England in the period 1540-1640, and the author also discusses the effect of the reduction in population caused by the ravages of the Black Death.

The Military Ratchet

"The military ratchet was the most important single influence in raising prices and reducing the value of money in the past 1,000 years, and for most of that time debasement was the most common, but not the only, way of strengthening the sinews of war." (page 646)

The financial consequences of Alexander the Great, the rise and fall of the Roman Empire, the Viking assault on England, the Norman Conquest, the Crusades, the Hundred Years War between England and France, the Spanish conquest of Mexico and Peru, the aftermath in Britain of the Napoleonic Wars, the U.S. Civil War, and the financing of the two World Wars are all treated.

The importance of war as a cause of inflation increased with the adoption of paper money in the west.

"When modern paper money release prices from their metallic anchors, the military ratchet began to be seen at its most powerful...The 'Continentals' of the new USA fell in value by the end of the Revolutionary War to one-thousandth of their nominal value, a process repeated by the Confederate paper which similarly became worthless by the end of the Civil War. The assignats of the French Revolution and the hyper-inflation of the German mark between 1918 and 1924 are simply among the best known of hundreds of examples of war-induced inflation." (page 647)

The Developmental Money Ratchet

"Second only to war as an engine of inflation is the general acceptance of the need for an ever-expanding supply of money in order to facilitate economic development, a belief which in a weaker and vaguer form long preceded the Keynesian revolution, though it was the Keynesian ratchet which acted as a strong causative factor in the unusually high peacetime inflations of the second half of the twentieth century." (page 647) Glyn Davies cites Sir William Petty and John Law, "the Keynes of the early eighteenth century", in this regard and discusses the fiasco of the Mississippi Bubble to show that the policy temptations facing politicians, governments and the public are not new. However, he also points out that in certain circumstances this ratchet can work and says "however much the Keynesian revolution may be condemned for its long-run consequences of high and stubborn inflation, Keynes's enormous success in providing cheap finance for the Second World War and in being largely responsible for the inestimable benefits of full employment for the first post-war generation, i.e. for its short- and medium-term benefits, should not be forgotten." (page 648).

Deflation

Sometimes the supply of money is insufficient to sustain economic activity at the level that would be reached if its productive capacity was fully utilized. Various instances are discussed in the book.

When Alexander the Great conquered the Persian empire he seized enormous quantities of precious metals which were melted down and used for making coins. Instead of causing inflation this gave a considerable boost to economic activity in the ancient world indicating the importance of coinage in revolutionising financial transactions.

Medieval England was much more successful than other major European countries in avoiding inflation, but the author points out that it could be argued that economic growth was sacrificed as a result though at this distance in time it is impossible to determine whether or not its economy was "crucified on a cross of silver" (to paraphrase the American politician William Jennings Bryan who in the presidential election campaign of 1896 made a famous speech about mankind being crucified on a cross of gold).

The British colonies in North America suffered greatly from a lack of official British coins and therefore adopted a variety of expedients including wampum, tobacco and paper money.

The Great Depression of the 1930s. One reason for its severity was the action of the FED in restricting the US money supply.

Pendulum Theory

As a result of the above-mentioned factors the supply of money tends to alternate in every age between too little and too much, with the pendulum swinging from excessive concern with the quality of money to the opposite extreme of an inflationary, excessive quantity of money.

This is the basis of the author's pendulum meta-theory of money, i.e. a "general theory comprising sets of more limited, partial theories, which spring out of the special circumstances of their time. The enveloping pendulum or metatheory also explains why the usual theories of money, despite being so confidently held at one time, tend to change so drastically and diametrically (and therefore so puzzlingly to the uninitiated) to an equally accepted but opposite theory within the time span appropriate to historical investigation." (pages 31-32).

In every age the supply of money tends to be either too generous or too restrictive, whether by objective standards or by those of creditors or debtors who have conflicting interests. According to the pendulum metatheory monetary theories do not deal with eternal verities but are prescriptions for courses of action that may be appropriate at particular times and places. Even when successful, by altering circumstances they ensure their own failure in the long term.

In support of these claims Glyn Davies ranges widely, both chronologically, from the dawn of civilization about 3000 BC onwards, and geographically from China to the New World, Denmark to Fiji. The development of financial policy and institutions in Britain, the United States, France, Germany and Japan is traced up to the present day. (The treatment of Britain and the United States is particularly detailed). There is also a chapter on the problems of the Third World. Thus a huge range of evidence regarding the causes of changes in both the quality and quantity of money is surveyed and the author concludes chapter 12, Global Money in Historical Perspective, with the words (from House of the Dead, part 1 chapter 2) of the Russian novelist Dostoevsky: "Money is coined liberty."

6

PRIMITIVE FORMS OF MONEY BANKING

INTRODUCTION

The use of primitive forms of money in the Third World and North America is more recent and better documented than in Europe and its study sheds light on the probable origins of modern money. Among the topics treated are the use of wampum and the custom of the potlatch or competitive gift exchange in North America, disc-shaped stones in Yap, cowrie shells over much of Africa and Asia, cattle, manillas and whales teeth.

Manillas were ornamental metallic objects worn as jewelry in west Africa and used as money as recently as 1949. They were an ostentatious form of ornamentation, their value in that role being a prime reason for their acceptability as money. Wampum's use as money in north America undoubtedly came about as an extension of its desirability for ornamentation. Precious metals have had ornamental uses throughout history and that could be one reason why they were adopted for use as money in many ancient societies and civilizations.

In Fijian society gifts of whales teeth were (and in certain cases still are) a significant feature of certain ceremonies. One of their uses was as bride-money, with a symbolic meaning similar to that of the engagement ring in Western society. Whales teeth were "tambua" (from which our word "taboo" comes) meaning that they had religious significance, as did the fei stones of Yap which were still being used as money as recently as the mid 1960s.

The potlatch ceremonies of Native Americans were a form of barter that had social and ceremonial functions that were at least as important as its economic functions. Consequently when the potlatch was outlawed in Canada (by an act that was later repealed) some of the most powerful work incentives were removed - to the detriment of the younger sections of the Indian communities. This form of barter was not unique to North America. Glyn Davies points out that the most celebrated example of competitive gift exchange was the encounter, around 950 BC, of Solomon and the Queen of Sheba. "Extravagant ostentation, the attempt to outdo each other in the splendour of the exchanges, and above all, the obligations of reciprocity, were just as typical in this celebrated encounter, though at a fittingly princely level, as with the more mundane types of barter in other parts of the world." (page 13).

Cattle are described by the author as mankind's "first working capital asset" (page 41). The religious use of cattle for sacrifices probably preceded their adoption for more general monetary purposes. For sacrifice quality - "without spot or blemish" - was important but for monetary purposes quantity was of more significance since cattle, like coins, can be counted. Obviously there were very practical reasons for the association between cattle and wealth but anthropological evidence from Africa in very recent times shows that when cattle are regarded as a form of money, not only health cattle but also scrawny ones will be valued to the detriment of the environment supporting them and their owners.

Glyn Davies quotes linguistic evidence to show how ancient and widespread the association between cattle and money was. The English words "capital", "chattels" and "cattle" have a common root. Similarly "pecuniary" comes from the Latin word for cattle "pecus" while in Welsh (the author's mother tongue) the word "da" used as an adjective means "good" but used as a noun means both "cattle" and "goods".

The author also cautions that "one should not confuse the abstract concept of an ox as a unit of account or standard of value, which is its essential but not only monetary function, with its admittedly cumbersome physical form. Once that is realized (a position quickly reached by primitive man if not yet by all economists or anthropologists), the inclusion of cattle as money is easily accepted, in practice and logic." (Page 41). He also points out that until well into the present century the Kirghiz of the Russian steppes used horses as their main monetary unit with sheep as a subsidiary unit. Small change was given in lambskins.

DEFINATION OF MONEY?

At first sight the answer to this question seems obvious; the man or woman in the street would agree on coins and banknotes, but would they accept them from any country? What about cheques? They would probably be less willing to accept them than their own country's coins and notes but bank money (i.e. anything for which you can write a cheque) actually accounts for by far the greatest proportion by value of the total supply of money. What about I.O.U.s (I owe you), credit cards and gold?

The gold standard belongs to history but even today in many rich people in different parts of the world would rather keep some of their wealth in the form of gold than in official, inflation-prone currencies. The attractiveness of gold, from an aesthetic point of view, and its resistance to corrosion are two of the properties which led to its use for monetary transactions for thousands of years. In complete contrast, a form of money with virtually no tangible properties whatsoever - electronic money - seems set to gain rapidly in popularity.

All sorts of things have been used as money at different times in different places. The alphabetical list below, taken from page 27 of A History of Money by Glyn Davies, includes but a minute proportion of the enormous variety of primitive moneys, and none of the modern forms.

Amber, beads, cowries, drums, eggs, feathers, gongs, hoes, ivory, jade, kettles, leather, mats, nails, oxen, pigs, quartz, rice, salt, thimbles, umiacs, vodka, wampum, yarns, and zappozats (decorated axes).

It is almost impossible to define money in terms of its physical form or properties since these are so diverse. Therefore any definition must be based on its functions.

FUNCTIONS OF MONEY

Specific functions (mostly micro-economic)

- Unit of account (abstract)
- Common measure of value (abstract)
- Medium of exchange (concrete)
- Means of payment (concrete)
- Standard for deferred payments (abstract)
- Store of value (concrete)

General functions (mostly macro-economic and abstract)

- Liquid asset
- Framework of the market allocative system (prices)
- A causative factor in the economy
- Controller of the economy

Not everything used as money as all the functions listed above. Furthermore the functions of any particular form of money may change over time. As Glyn Davies points out on page 28:

"What is now the prime or main function in a particular community or country may not have been the first or original function in time, while what may well have been a secondary or derived function in one place may have been in some other region the original which gave rise to a related secondary function... The logical listing of functions in the table therefore implies no priority in either time or importance, for those which may be both first and foremost reflect only their particular time and place."

He goes on to conclude from this that the best definition is as follows:

Money is anything that is widely used for making payments and accounting for debts and credits.

Causes of the Development of Money

In his preface the author writes:

"Money originated very largely from non-economic causes: from tribute as well as from trade, from blood-money and bride-money as well as from barter, from ceremonial and religious rites as well as from commerce, from ostentatious ornamentation as well as from acting as the common drudge between economic men."

One of the most important improvements over the simplest forms of early barter was the tendency to select one or two items in preference to others so that the preferred items became partly accepted because of their qualities in acting as media of exchange. Commodities were chosen as preferred barter items for a number of reasons - some because they were conveniently and easily stored, some because they had high value densities and were easily portable, and some because they were durable. These commodities, being widely desired, would be easy to exchange for others and therefore they came to be accepted as money.

To the extent that the disadvantages of barter provided an impetus for the development of money that impetus was purely economic but archaeological, literary and linguistic evidence of the ancient world, and the tangible evidence of actual types of primitive money from many countries demonstrate that barter was not the main factor in the origins and earliest development of money.

Many societies had laws requiring compensation in some form for crimes of violence, instead of the Old Testament approach of "an eye for an eye". The author notes that the word to "pay" is derived from the Latin "pacare" meaning originally to pacify, appease, or make peace with - through the appropriate unit of value customarily acceptable to both sides. A similarly widespread custom was payment for brides in order to compensate the head of the family for the loss of a daughter's services. Rulers have since very ancient times imposed taxes on or exacted tribute from their subjects. Religious obligations might also entail payment of tribute or sacrifices of some kind. Thus in many societies there was a requirement for a means of payment for blood-money, bride-money, tax or tribute and this gave a great impetus to the spread of money.

Objects originally accepted for one purpose were often found to be useful for other non-economic purposes and, because of their growing acceptability began to be used for general trading also, supplementing or replacing barter.

Thus the use of money evolved out of deeply rooted customs; the clumsiness of barter provided an economic impulse but that was not the primary factor. It evolved independently in different parts of the world. About the only civilization that functioned without money was that of the Incas.

MONETARY INNOVATION IN HISTORICAL PERSPECTIVE

Money, the quintessential Great Communicator and Great Survivor, has been talking with growing authority and, despite occasional backsliding, to an ever wider, richer audience since the dawn of civilisation. Modern research confirms Keynes's belief that "Money is a far more ancient institution than we were taught to believe some few years ago. Its origins are lost in the mists when the ice was melting, and may well stretch back into the paradisaic intervals in human history of the inter-glacial periods, when the weather was delightful and the mind free to be fertile of new ideas in the Islands of the Hesperides or Atlantis or some Eden of Central Asia." (Keynes, J.M.(1930) Treatise on Money, v.i., p. 13, Macmillan).

Money has survived and developed, with attractively vigorous arrogance, for over 6,000 years because it has very carefully tried to combine eager acceptability and flexible adaptability on the one hand, integrally with the opposite but complementary attributes of stability and authority on the other hand. Success spirals, then fails. Whenever that linkage slips, or snaps as in repeated financial crises, we are forced to relearn, preferably from past history, how to rebuild a more stable monetary system.

Sometimes it is the accelerating, innovative forces making for greater flexibility and faster economic growth that are responsible for the breakdown of the monetary system, either through long term inflation or through the more extreme but unfortunately still common case of a sudden bubble. At other times over-emphasis on stability by the monetary authorities or social inertia tend to depress long term growth far below its potential - as in all of Europe in the 1930s and in most of Euro-obsessed Continental Europe today. This 20th century pattern repeats the neglected experience of previous ages, perhaps as far back as when global warming was a happy spur to innovation and not the harbinger of a new doomsday.

Positive turning points leading to sustained periods of rapid economic growth occur from time to time, particularly when technical innovations, e.g. in mining techniques,, combine with a supportive or expanding state authority. In such favourable circumstances the monetary consequences may then well become truly revolutionary.

Examples range from the land-base empires of Alexander and Rome to the world's most extensive sea-based British Empire, culminating in the apparently ideal international gold standard based on the pound sterling. No one in this audience, and few outside can dispute that we are now poised at such a revolutionary turning point. The following startling statement made recently by two expert monetary analysts may not be an exaggeration:

"Technical innovation, the massive scale on which transactions are now occurring and irreversible trends to financial deregulation and commercial globalisation mean the current decade will see more change in international payment systems than the preceding millennium". (Wood, D. & Erturk, I.(1996), European Payment Systems; p. 7-8, Payment, Past, Present & Future, APACS).

Before glancing at a few of the more outstanding turning points it is advisable to remind ourselves of some of the enduring monetary fundamentals which channel, limit and sometimes reverse the forces of financial revolution. Inertia among the more numerous users of traditional forms of money usually delays acceptance of the new.

HISTORY PROVIDES A FRUITFUL MONETARY LABORATORY

Money is much more than a technical device or a mere commercial lubricant. It has, right from its varied beginnings, exhibited strong socio-political attributes. Rarely does money operate in a social vacuum. Because money is used daily by everybody changes which may appear to be purely technical not infrequently turn out to have unexpected serious social, political and constitutional consequences.

Today, when national sovereignties are threatened by e-moneys - whether regional Euros or global Electronic - that fact is forcing itself with awkward insistence, on public attention. But this in essence is nothing new. From earliest times money in some form or another has been central to organised living. Increasingly it moulds the economic and foreign policies of all governments. It is synonymous with power and shapes history in every generation.

In our technological age too many agree with Henry Ford's dictum that history is bunk, though he was far from thinking that money was bunk. Because of the difficulties of conducting experiments in the ordinary business of economic life, at the centre of which is money, it is most fortunate that history generously provides us with a potentially plentiful proxy laboratory where alternative policies may be analysed. Around the next corner there may be lying in wait apparently quite novel monetary problems which in all probability bear a basic similarity to those that have already been tackled with varying degrees of success or failure in other times and places.

Many economists, especially monetarists, tend to overestimate the purely commercial, narrow, technical functions of money and place insufficient emphasis on its wider social and psychological aspects. Yet money originated very largely from non-commercial causes: from tribute as well as trade, from blood-money and bride-money as well as from barter, from ceremonial and religious rites as well as from acting as the common drudge between economic men. Money, more than ever in our monetarist era (and policy lags behind theory), needs to be widely interpreted to include not only currency and banking, but also savings banks, building societies (if any), hire-purchase companies etc. In particular the fiscal framework frequently complements or conflicts with monetary policy. The Maastricht convergence criteria, with their emphasis on fiscal rectitude, reflect the long-ingrained habits of governments to fudge- i.e. to beg, borrow or steal as an alternative to simply printing money.

Even in medieval and earlier periods these wider aspects were of considerably greater importance than is conventionally assumed. There are therefore many insights to be gained from looking back at past monetary developments, where so-called primitive and modern moneys have overlapped for centuries and where the logical and chronological progressions have rarely followed strictly parallel paths. Even the most advanced experts should never neglect the rear driving mirror, nor the old bag of tools back in the boot.

SOME SIGNIFICANT TURNING POINTS

From among the many outstanding innovations which have radically changed the way we use money - and therefore the way we live - the following few examples are taken. First comes the invention of hammered coinage; secondly the invention of printing and its long-delayed application to bank notes; and thirdly, and perhaps most surprisingly, the slow emergence of simple, non-technical changes in accounting practices, even when some of these have depended on the use of the most ancient of devices.

Coins Give the Midas Touch to Economic History

In chronology China comes first, its miniature tool money mouldings appearing in common use, guaranteed by the state, by about the end of the second millennium B.C. However, in quality, range of functions and influence on the rest of the world, Lydia as the birthplace and Ionian Greece as the nursery of coined money have undoubted priority over China. Literally, at a stroke, markets were speeded up and vastly extended: in a word, revolutionised. The chronology of Lydian and early Greek coinage has undergone thorough revision recently, the result of which is to accelerate the speed of change from crudity to perfection. "The extraordinary characteristic of Greek coinage is the speed with which it developed... By 550 B.C. the techniques were still primitive, (yet) the fifth century saw the minting of the most beautiful coins ever made." (Price, M.J., The First Three Centuries of Coinage).

Historians need to put in a good word for numismatists for they help to bring the past vividly to life. A brilliant instance of this took place at an auction at Sotheby's in July 1995 of some 200 ancient coins, estimated to fetch £1½m. but actually realizing over £2m. One single coin, minted in 460 B.C., went for £132,000. These costly examples eloquently remind us that for most of the last 2,700 years coins have been by far the most important form of money. At the end of the twentieth century it is, surprisingly, still true that more coins are being produced and put into daily use by more people around the world than ever before. In the struggle for the retail market Mondex, Digicash and their like face the entrenched defences of the longest-lived, most tried and tested kind of money known to civilised society.

For the vast majority of people coins remained by far the most important form of money , right up to 1914. (Scotland was an enlightened exception). British public policy in 1913 was still absolutely convinced on the virtues of gold coinage and wished to extend its apparently obvious benefits to India. This spurred the young Keynes into revolt against the majority conclusions of Austin Chamberlain's Royal Commission on Indian Currency and Finance. The world should not leave "the most intimate adjustment of our economic organism at the mercy of a lucky prospector, a new chemical process, or a change of ideas in Asia", (Keynes, J.M. 1913, Indian Currency and Finance p.101, Macmillan).

It was not however the exasperation of Keynes but the exigencies of war which just one year later led to the strategic turning point in the direction to which Keynes was pointing, for gold was withdrawn from circulation in most countries during the war of 1914-18.

"Thus the long age of Commodity Money has at last passed away". By 1923, two years before Britain's abortive return to the gold standard, the precious metal had been prophetically and permanently devalued by Keynes: "In truth, the gold standard is already a barbarous relic" (1931 Essays in Persuasion, p. 184 & 208, Macmillan). So all coins now (with a few relatively unimportant exceptions) are not only mere tokens - but they are also of ever-diminishing importance in the total money supply. In the mid 1990s coins come to only one-tenth of notes and only one three-hundredth part of U.K.'s broad money, M4.

Yet in a perverse burst of energy they still defy their long announced death sentence. Macro-economically speaking they have a low, but still positive national income elasticity of demand. (Translation: countries want more coins). Thus the Report of the Royal Mint for 1993-4 shows that "the production of blanks and coins (at 3.5 billion), operating profit and export sales (to some 70 countries) were all substantially in excess of the best achieved in its long history" of over a thousand years.

This surge will be eclipsed by the huge demand for the new Euro coins required by 2002. Even allowing for considerable slippage, the prospect discloses an unprecedentedly large, contemporaneous demand for coins by up to 370 million customers in the next decade. (For further details on the urgent planning for the Euro, see the frenetic pronouncements of, e.g. the Cees Maas Report (10 May 1995) of the Expert Group on the Changeover to the Single Currency, and One Currency for Europe (21 May 1995), the Green Paper on the Practical Arrangements for the Introduction of the Single Currency).

Incidentally, the bland designs for the euro currency, typical of the bloodless bureaucrats of Brussels, are obviously based on the belief that money is merely a technical device - a vivid contrast with the patriotic mottoes and emblems carried by coins ever since their creation. "I will conquer Greece with my archers", boasted the Persian kings, only to be overcome by the owls of Athens. Perhaps our Europhobes can see a hidden inscription: "I shall conquer England - or at least the City of London - with my euros". In reply our wise owls simply sit on the fence. The monetary reforms in the former Soviets point to similar substantial increases in new coinage, though, as in EC, politics, not economics, will be the deciding factor: what's new? Between 1993 and 1995 the Royal Mint had already found customers in Estonia, Mongolia, Turkmenistan, Croatia and the Czech Republic. In its Report for 1996-97, after drawing attention to "a surprising and remarkable growth in demand" (of over 23.5%) for U.K. coins it goes on to show that, as "the world leader in the circulating coin market" it is well placed to meet demand for the euro as well as that from the Third World.

It is this latter demand which, over time, is likely to be the largest of all, for a number of reasons. In economic terms coins are not merely inferior goods but also exhibit Giffen tendencies, where an individual's demand falls when incomes rise. Thus, above a very low threshold, the demand for coins by the poor tends to be much higher than that by richer people who have access to many other forms of payment. Secondly the size and rate of growth of population in poor countries far exceeds on average that in richer areas. Thirdly, allied to the above, is the younger age distribution in most poor countries. Fourthly, the infrastructural assets e.g. telecommunications essential for the full development of non-cash systems are not as available or as reliable as in rich nations.

Fifthly, the reduction in inflation to what is believed to be sustainably and substantially lower levels than in previous years makes it economic, in view of their much greater durability, to withdraw small denomination bank notes in favour of new coins. Yet, as we have already noted, despite this enormous increase coins are more than ever merely the very small change in a modern country's total money supply, where abstract forms predominate.

Printing versus Minting : a Classic 'Sailing-ship Effect'

Gutenberg was a brilliant inventor ... but not much good with money, being forced to accept finance from an overbearing local banker in order to launch the world's first book (with movable type) the Great Psalter, in Mainz in 1457. Its impact was truly revolutionary, acting as the engine of the Renaissance, with 1,700 printing presses turning out around twenty million books by the end of the century.

The connection between the new invention and monetary innovation is however startlingly different from what might logically have been expected. Gutenberg cannot be blamed for the inflationary sins of subsequent generations of note makers obsessed with the limitless potential of the printing press. Historical progress laughs at the locksmiths of arid academic logic and frequently demonstrates a fascinating perversity in apparently backing the wrong horses with the wrong money.

If the historical progress of money had followed the logical steps assumed by, among others, some of the fashionable alternative historians, then Gutenberg's invention would quickly have brought about the triumph of printed over minted money. It took not decades, but rather hundreds of years for this logical conclusion to establish itself.

In actual fact, in an early but classic example of what later became known as the sailing-ship effect, the powerful new presses then being developed, of which printing was but one type, led first to a revolution in minting to provide coins in quantities with less cost and human effort than before.

Leonardo da Vinci, a young contemporary of Gutenberg, produced detailed designs for mechanised minting to produce faster and more uniform coins, including a water-powered mill driving seven hammers, a pattern later adopted by the goldsmiths and coiners of Augsburg and Nuremberg to produce the remarkably fine coins known as milled. The indentations made possible by such stronger presses gave rise to the milled-edge coin giving greater protection against clipping - hence the motto "Decus et Tutamen" (an Ornament and a Safeguard). The making of milled money spread via Paris to the Tower mint by 1553, though it was not until the 1630s that the first substantial amount of milled money was produced, in Britain.

By that time the London goldsmiths were about to emerge as bankers. With the founding of the Bank of England in 1694 and the early prominence it gave to note issue (compared with other banks), the total quantity of abstract paper money was eventually beginning to show its irreversible pattern of exceeding in an increasing degree that of solid, concrete, hard cash. All the same, for the next two hundred years the true value of this inverted pyramid of money was deemed to rest upon a metallic foundation the essential ingredient of which was the circulation of full-bodied gold coinage, supplemented by the remarkably thin reserves of the Bank of England.

The vast superstructure of abstract money rested, right up until 1914, on this solid, traditional golden foundation. And we, still worry about sending our gold reserves - and our sovereignty - to Frankfurt, the Fort Knox of the EU.

Really Creative Accounting

Some of the most important changes in the monetary basis of our economy have come about, not as the result of dramatic inventions like the printing press, computer or laser, but simply through gradual, humdrum modifications in the use of money in carrying out its age-old function of being a unit of account in which debts and credits are calculated. Our first example is the development of double-entry bookkeeping, originating in the cradle of Renaissance Italy, popularised by the first printed book on the subject by a close friend of Leonardo da Vinci, Friar Luca Pacioli, published in 1494. While allowing for some exaggeration the point was well put by Werner Sombart: "Capitalism without double-entry bookkeeping is simply inconceivable ... With this way of thinking the concept of capital is first created". (see my History of Money 234-50).

Our second example is the tally. From time immemorial notched sticks had been used for keeping a record of messages, especially payments, but nowhere did the use of the tally develop to such an extent as in Britain, even after the arrival of modern banking methods and cheap paper had long rendered them redundant.

One authority on the history of the Treasury has stated that "English medieval finance was built upon the tally" (Steel, A. 1954, The Receipt of the Exchequer 1377-1485, Cambridge). It developed into a sort of wooden bill of exchange, helped to build up an embryo money market in London and thus effectively considerably increased the money supply beyond the limits of minting.

Almost incredibly the Treasury Tally lasted officially until 1826 when masses of redundant tallies were stored in the House of Commons. In 1834, to save space and economise on fuel they were fed into the ovens.

"So excessive was the zeal of the stokers that the historic Parliament buildings were set on fire and razed to the ground. The tallies perished in a blaze of defiant glory" (see my History of Money pp. 147-52, 251-2, 663). This backward glance is a further reminder that fundamental monetary changes rarely leave the political constitution unmoved: perhaps the computer will chip away what remains of Parliamentary sovereignty in matters of finance.

When official money was made only by the monarch then controlling it was conceptually simple, though even then difficult in practice, for there always tended to be too much or too little in relation to changing demands. Furthermore the government's supposed monopoly was always threatened by competition - by counterfeiters, dealers in bills of exchange and increasingly from the seventeenth century onwards by banks whose money-creating powers eventually came to dominate the total money supply. In these circumstances governments were reduced to trying to control the quantity and quality of moneys created mainly by others - in effect by any Tom, Dick or Harriet in banks scattered around the country, responsive to local businesses, not centralised in London. The Bank of England did this very successfully between 1844 and 1914 through Bank Rate and Open Market Operations. Afterwards these worked badly.

Although the power of bad money over good had been observed from the time of Aristophanes (405 B.C.) - and therefore the essence of the quantity theory of money, - it was not (incredible as it may seem) until 1970 that official money supply figures were published by the Bank. Even then they failed at first to include the deposits in building societies, despite the fact their retail savings exceeded those in the banks, that the societies were growing daily more bank-like and were repeating the history, a century later, of indulging in a merger mania bound to lead to a more integrated and potentially more inflationary financial system. Belatedly and hesitatingly building society deposits were included as the Bank experimented in producing a rash of money supply definitions - Ml, M2, M3, Sterling M3, M3C, M4, M4C, M5, PSL1, PSL2, DCE etc. - surely a case of the uncontrollable in pursuit of the indefinable. Inflation running at 27% in the mid 1970s proved that if anyone was in control of the money supply it was brother Jack Jones of the TGW Union and not the then Governor of the Bank of England, Sir Gordon Richardson.

Subsequently, thanks to Thatcherism, Reaganomics, recession and a more mature realisation by the public of the evils of inflation, by the mid 1990s inflation in most advanced countries seemed to be well under control. However, widespread "fudging" by the major European governments in order to meet the Maastricht convergence criteria is simply a macro-economic variant of old-fashioned currency debasement, such as can weaken the credibility of even the apparently strongest currency (see the Monthly Bulletin, Deutsche Bundesbank, June 1997, p. 5-7, for its spirited attack on Chancellor Kohl's request for it to re-value its gold reserves, deeming this unequivocally as "an infringement of the Bundesbank's independence" and "counter to German tradition".

Stable money requires eternal vigilance by the monetary authorities together with - vitally - the co-operation of an informed public who handle powerful new tools. Billions of fingers, at the touch of a button in a borderless world, will keep the august monetary authorities on their toes, as new definitions of money, of monetary sovereignty and control will be dictated by the as yet unknown demands of the electronic age. For the computer chip with its phenomenal memory enables us practically to turn Blake's poetic vision into virtual reality:

To see a world in a grain of sand ...

Hold infinity in the palm of your hand

And eternity in an hour.

VIOLENCE AND THE ORIGIN OF MONEY

Many societies had laws requiring compensation in some form for crimes of violence, instead of the Old Testament approach of "an eye for an eye". The author notes that the word to "pay" is derived from the Latin "pacare" meaning originally to pacify, appease, or make peace with - through the appropriate unit of value customarily acceptable to both sides. Objects originally accepted for one purpose were often found to be useful for others and, because of their growing acceptability began to be used for general trading also. Thus the practice of paying compensation for certain crimes was one of the factors that played a role in the origins of money.

Ever since the invention of coins monetary and military history have been inter-related to a degree that is both depressing and surprising. Glyn Davies goes so far as to paraphrase Clausewitz's famous dictum and refer to war as the continuation of monetary policy by other means, and quotes a

of annual budgets, and a prices and incomes policy. Thus there was a shift from a market economy in the direction of a controlled one. Diocletian's successor Constantine continued his reforms and also introduced new gold coins and ensured that there was a plentiful supply for the influential sections of Roman society.

The measures undertaken by these two emperors did not eradicate inflation but they did enable Rome to live with it, ensuring the survival of the western empire until the 5th century and laying the foundations of the eastern or Byzantine empire. The army and the bureaucracy were kept happy while welfare payments helped to keep the poorest sections of society from causing trouble. Nevertheless Rome was seriously weakened by inflation before it fell to the Barbarians.

Anglo-Saxon and Viking Invasions of Britain

The effect of the fall of Rome was particularly marked in Britain where money virtually disappeared from use for a couple of centuries, the island reverting to barter. Later, after the Anglo-Saxon invaders started to mint coins (originally by copying those made in France) they had in their turn to face invaders from the east - the Vikings.

This led to a immense increase in the minting of coins in England because of the demand for Danegeld to pay the invaders to go home, or heregeld, a tax to pay for the armies of those monarchs who chose to fight the Vikings.

Huge quantities of English coins from this period have been found in Scandinavia. After Athelstan reconquered the Danelaw he passed the Statute of Greatley in 928 which established a single national currency for England and marked the start of the unbroken 1,000 year history of the pound sterling. Later monarchs relied more on their mints than their armies to defend the realm. Aethelred's 75 mints coined nearly 40 million silver pennies for the payment of Danegeld.

One linguistic legacy of the Viking era is the phrase "to pay through the nose". This expression comes from the unfortunate habit of the Danes in Ireland in the 9th century who slit the noses of those unwilling or unable to pay the Danish poll tax.

The Norman Conquest

William the Conqueror financed the Norman invasion and conquest of England partly by debasing Norman currency. However, he resisted the temptation to do the same to the English coinage and instead raised revenue through the introduction of new taxes. The very detailed survey of the resources of his new kingdom, recorded in the Domesday Book, facilitated the imposition of these taxes.

Furthermore, the tax collectors would naturally reject below-weight or impure coins and thus the system of taxation not only provided an alternative to debasement but also gave the rulers an incentive to maintain the quality of the coinage and so the value of English money remained remarkably stable for several centuries, in marked contrast to the situation on the Continent.

The Crusades and the Re-Emergence of Banking

Before the time of Henry II it was normal in England, as in other feudal countries, for the the king's tenants-in-chief and their retainers to owe him a period of military service, usually 40 days annually. Henry replaced this obligation with cash payments known as scutage and used the money to pay for a permanent professional army of mercenaries or soldiers as they commonly became known after this time from the solidus or king's shilling that they earned. England's participation in the Crusades required additional expenditure which Henry II financed by levying heavy taxes on all movable property and all incomes.

But, although huge sums accumulated in Henry's eastern account he refused to let anyone spend them until after the disastrous battle of Hattin in 1187. Thus the loss of much of the Holy Land to Saladin was due to the miserly restrictions placed by Henry on the use of his vast hoard of money in a vain attempt to have his cake and eat it.

Henry's successor, Richard I (the "Lion Heart") raised money for the 3rd Crusade partly by the sale of as many publicly owned assets as possible (a measure which the author compares to Margaret Thatcher's "privatization" policy in the 1980s which has been copied by governments around the world). On his return journey he was captured in Vienna and imprisoned by Emperor Henry VI. The ransom demanded far exceeded the average revenue of the Kingdom of England but nevertheless a high proportion of it was raised quite quickly (through special taxes and gifts) and he was released.

Payments for supplies, equipment, allies, ransoms etc. required safe and speedy means of transferring vast resources of cash. Consequently the Knights of the Temple and the Hospitallers began to provide some banking services such as those already being developed in some of the Italian city states where the need to transfer sums of money for trading purposes led to the development of financial services including bills of exchange. Banking had been invented in the Middle East long before the invention of coins but was abandoned and forgotten after the collapse of the Roman empire. The Crusades gave a great stimulus to its re-emergence.

The Spanish Conquest of Mexico and Peru

The Spanish conquests in the New World were, like the Crusades, partly motivated by missionary zeal but also by greed. The Europe of the Middle Ages had often experienced shortages of bullion but with the conquest of the Aztecs in Mexico and the Incas in Peru, and the opening of the silver mines in Potosi (now in Bolivia) the dearth gave way to abundance leading to problems of inflation in Europe.

The repercussions of the Spanish conquests were felt as far away as China. Initially imports of silver from the New World gave a boost to the Chinese economy but eventually the country became dangerously dependent on that source for its basic monetary supplies.

The stage was reached when the total annual output of China's own silver mines was less than that carried in a single Spanish galleon sailing from Acapulco. As a result, when bullion imports started to dry up after 1640 the Chinese economy, the world's largest, was plunged into a terrible recession which undermined the stability of the Ming Empire (1368-1644).

Francis Drake and the Spanish Armada

During Francis Drake's circumnavigation of the globe 1577-1580, booty estimated at between £ 300,000 and £ 1,500,000 was seized from the Spaniards. According to John Maynard Keynes:

The booty brought back by Drake in the Golden Hind may fairly be considered the fountain and origin of British Foreign Investment. ... In view of this, the following calculation may amuse the curious. At the present time (in round figures) our foreign investments probably yield us about 6½ per cent net after allowing for losses, of which we reinvest abroad about half - say 3¼ per cent. If this is, on average, a fair sample of what has been going on since 1580, the £ 42,000 invested by Elizabeth out of Drake's booty in 1580 would have accumulated by 1930 to approximately the actual aggregate of our present foreign investments, namely £ 4,200,000,000 - or say 100,000 times greater than the original investment.

Several years after his epic voyage Drake and his fellow Sea Dogs were in action against the Spanish Armada. Atrocious weather in the summer of 1588 helped to seal the Armada's fate but it is possible that things might have worked out differently if it had been able to sail earlier. The previous year, agents acting for Sir Francis Walsingham, Elizabeth l's secretary of state and spymaster, are reputed to have cornered large numbers of bills drawn on Genoan banks in order to delay the build up of resources to equip the Spanish fleet - an early example of economic warfare.

The English Civil War 1642-1651

This war broke out because parliament disputed the king's right to levy taxes without its consent. The use of goldsmith's safes as secure places for people's jewels, bullion and coins increased after the seizure of the mint by Charles I in 1640 and increased again with the outbreak of the Civil War. Consequently some goldsmiths became bankers and development of this aspect of their business continued after the Civil War was over. Within a few years of the victory by the parliamentary forces, written instructions to goldsmiths to pay money to another customer had developed into the cheque (or check in American spelling). Goldsmiths' receipts were used not only for withdrawing deposits but also as evidence of ability to pay and by about 1660 these had developed into the banknote.

War of the League of Augsburg and the War of the Spanish Succession

In addition to taxation (and sometimes debasement of coinage) wars were financed by borrowing. This was one of the motives behind the establishment of the Bank of England in 1694. At that time the British government was desperately short of cash for the war against Louis XIV, the most powerful ruler in Europe. The lending resources of the goldsmiths combined with taxation, including new forms of taxation copied largely from the Dutch, could not supply the money needed. If the British government could raise a perpetual loan at a rate of interest acceptable to it, then instead of having to repay the capital only the interest would ever be repaid and the additional taxation required at any time would be just a fraction of the total loan. The lenders agreed to these terms because of various benefits to themselves that were attached to the deal. This, and other official borrowings, formed the "national debt" because it was not the personal debt of the monarch, which might be repudiated as Charles II did with his infamous "Stop of the Exchequer", but the debt of the government itself, guaranteed by parliament.

The role of the Bank of England was not confined simply to enabling the government to raise the money needed for the prosecution of the war. Michael Godfrey, the Bank's deputy governor (who was killed by a French cannonball during the siege of Namur in 1695) succeeded in establishing a system whereby the army received its funds promptly, (in marked contrast to the situation that prevailed during Henry II's participation in the 2nd Crusade when failure to make the money available in time was a major factor in the defeat by Saladin). After an interval of 4 years of peace a fresh war against Louis XIV broke out, the war of the Spanish Succession, and Britain and her allies were completely victorious, thanks largely to the military genius of John Churchill, Duke of Marlborough (an ancestor of Winston Churchill).

Anglo-French Wars in North America

In 1690 the first official state issue of paper money was made by the Massachusetts Bay Colony. These notes, amounting to £ 40,000 and promising eventual redemption in gold or silver, were issued to pay soldiers returning from an expedition to Quebec. A chronic shortage of official British coins caused other colonies to follow this example. Over-issuing of notes caused inflation but attempts by the British government to restrict the use of paper money caused considerable resentment.

Competition between the British colonies for Spanish silver coins pushed up their market rate causing problems in obtaining military provisions. Inflation was blamed for the lack of equipment and the delays which led to the defeat of General Braddock at Fort Duquesne in 1755. General Wolfe also complained of a lack of funds in his successful Quebec campaign in 1759. These complaints stiffened the British government's determination to increase taxation and revenue in America, so spurring the Revolution.

The American Revolution

The importance of war as a cause of inflation increased with the adoption of paper money in the west. Because of a general shortage of currency in the British colonies in north America, many of the colonies started to issue paper money. As these issues were often excessive, causing inflation, the British government acted at first to restrict and then to forbid the issue of paper money and this was one of the many acts of interference which caused the resentment which led, eventually, to the American Revolution. When the war broke out the monetary brakes were released completely and the revolution was financed overwhelmingly with an expansionary flood of paper money and so the American Congress financed its first war with hyperinflation.

By the end of the war the "Continentals" had fallen to one-thousandth of their nominal value. Yet although the phrase "not worth a Continental" has subsequently symbolized utter worthlessness, in the perspective of economic history such notes should be counted as invaluable as being the only major practical means then available for financing the successful revolution.

The Napoleonic Wars

Britain was the first country to undergo the Industrial Revolution. It was already well underway when the Napoleonic Wars broke out and was a factor in Britain's economic strength. Much of the working capital required by the new enterprises was supplied by the commercial banks which had emerged to supply the needs of various regions and Glyn Davies asserts that "without the banks the revolution would have been strangled in its infancy" (page 292).

In addition to greatly increasing expenditure on Britain's own armed forces, William Pitt, the prime minister, sent large subsidies to Britain's allies, a total of more than 15 million Pounds between 1793 and 1801, including a loan of 1,200,000 Pounds to Austria in July 1796. In 1797, after a run on the Bank of England triggered off by an abortive French landing in Pembrokeshire, the Bank's notes were made inconvertible.

Between 1783 and 1816 the National Debt rose from 273 million to 816 million Pounds. In addition to long term borrowing Pitt raised funds by introducing income tax, at a rate of 10%, and widening indirect taxes as far as possible.

During the Napoleonic wars Britain experienced a certain amount of inflation which, despite being of a rather modest degree, was worrying to contemporary observers who were used to stable prices and an official inquiry blamed the Bank of England for issuing too much credit. As a result Britain adopted the gold standard for the Pound after the wars were over in 1816.

The War of 1812

After the revolution one might have expected the newly independent Americans to have welcomed with enthusiasm their freedom to set up banks but in fact there was a great deal of opposition to banking in general. The first true American bank, the Bank of North America had its congressional charter repealed in 1785. The first national bank, the Bank of the United States, though a financial success, was forced to close when its charter was not renewed. As a result, when the 1812 War broke out there was no government bank to exert a restraining hand on the commercial banks which issued far too many notes backed by far too little specie and the American financial scene reverted to its familiar inflationary pattern.

After the 1812 War the Second Bank of the United States was set up but once one of the heroes of that war, General Jackson, became president it was doomed to failure. Jackson admitted to Nicholas Biddle, the last president of the Bank, "ever since I read the history of the South Sea Bubble I have been afraid of banks." By killing the Second Bank Jackson delayed the establishment of a sensibly regulated banking system for eighty years.

The US Civil War

The war required a rapid transfer of resources from diffused and decentralized civilian expenditure to concentrated and centrally controlled military expenditure, by means of some combination of taxing, borrowing and printing money. The mixture actually chosen differed markedly between the Unionists and the Confederates.

The Union government levied two direct taxes; the first was on each of the states in proportion to population rather than ability to pay and it was therefore regarded as unfair by the poorer states. Rather better yields were obtained by a general income tax but even so these two taxes together yielded less than $200 million. Much more important were indirect taxes which at their maximum rates yielded over a billion dollars. Initial attempts at long term borrowing were not very successful but after an Ohio banker, Jay Cooke, was put in charge of marketing bonds an issue of $500 million was oversubscribed by the public. During 1863 and 1864 another $900 million were issued but the low interest rate no longer appealed to the public and so the Union had to rely on the assistance of the banks to ensure the sale of the debt instruments.

The North's record on inflation stands up well in comparison with the experience of victorious countries in later wars, even though the Greenbacks' (inconvertible notes issued by the Union government) worth in gold fell to half their nominal value.

In the South the imposition of adequate taxes and their collection was a case of too little too late. The Confederacy's borrowing policy was more successful than its taxation policies but was still inadequate. The Southern states relied on Europe's dependence on "King Cotton" to raise loans of $15 million but because of the blockade only around a quarter of the expected supplies came from such sources.

The one seemingly unlimited resource was the printing press and hyperinflation resulted from its use. The South could probably at best only have moderated hyperinflation to a limited degree as the mix of fiscal and financial policies available to the Union was just not possible for the Confederacy to put into effect.

The Franco - Prussian War 1870-1871

In the same year as their victory over France the German states united to form a single country and adopted the Mark as their common currency, basing it on the gold standard which had already been in use by Britain for decades. Other countries followed the German example leading to the abandonment of bimetallism and the gold standard becoming an international one. The demonetization of silver by European countries was partly responsible for an increase in the amount of silver available in world markets. Consequently countries which still depended on silver for their currencies such as India, China and Japan suffered from inflation. The victorious Germans forced France to pay a huge indemnity of 5 billion francs. The money was raised easily by a loan which was more than 10 times oversubscribed. This experience partly explains French reliance on borrowing in preference to taxation in the First World War and French insistence on German reparations afterwards.

1st World War

Lloyd George, as chancellor of the exchequer, was responsible for a revolutionary series of budgets from 1909-1911, introducing far greater progression into the financial system, tapping far more copiously the wealth of the rich.

The author writes: "although the purpose of Lloyd George's fiscal policy was for financing social welfare benefits the fiscal framework had thereby been fundamentally transformed on the eve of the First World War into a much more buoyant source of revenue, ripe for the insatiable demands of the military machine.

What had been introduced at the cost of a seething constitutional crisis, for welfare became a timely godsend for warfare." (page 369)

Even so the scale of expenditure so alarmed Keynes that he warned of the danger of Britain becoming bankrupt by the spring of 1916. This did not happen. As in previous wars old taxes were increased and new ones were introduced. Huge loans were also raised, including the first billion pound loan in world history.

However the British government failed to use its monopsonistic power as the only purchaser of really large loans in wartime to get such loans at a cheap rate. Britain also raised loans abroad, borrowing 1,365 million Pounds chiefly from the USA but that was more than offset by Britain's loans to its allies, a total of 1,741 million Pounds.

After the war Germany has difficulty in making its agreed reparations and experiences hyperinflation from 1922-1923.

Later, in the 1930s the social turmoil resulting from mass unemployment results in Hitler's installation as Chancellor.

Second World War

"By the beginning of the Second World War Keynes's ideas had already so permeated Whitehall and Westminster that high interest rates were rejected as unnecessary, costly and perverse" (page 391). Glyn Davies describes the various ingenious methods adopted by the government to raise money at low rates of interest.

"With just a few unimportant exceptions, 3 percent became in fact the maximum rate at which the government borrowed within the United Kingdom" (page 391). "The most grievously costly war in history, in real, human terms was thus financed by incredibly cheap money. The financial lessons of all previous wars had been the more you borrow the higher the rate. The revolution in economic thought led by Keynes had helped the government to borrow far more money than ever before at rates of interest far lower than ever before in such circumstances." (page 393)

The US government also succeeded in keeping interest rates low with the Fed strongly supporting the seven War Loans and the Victory Loan. During the 1930s the New Deal had required a new banking system to restore business confidence in order to revive industry and agriculture and reduce America's appalling total of 13 million unemployed. The first relief agency (which had already been set up by President Hoover in 1932) was the Reconstruction Finance Corporation which played an important role not only in the recovery from the Depression but also supplied vitally needed investment for military purposes during the War.

From $16 million in 1930 the national debt rose to $269 million in 1946. This immense increase in borrowing was accomplished at very low interest rates (2.5% or less). Direct controls on credit were introduced, and physical controls and rationing, though nothing like as severe as in Britain, suppressed most of the inflation until after the war ended.

After its defeat, For the second time in a generation Germany experienced hyperinflation. In Hungary hyperinflation was the worst in world history. Many European countries introduced new reformed currencies in the years after the war.

CONCLUSION

As a result of his survey of the history of money the author concludes:

> "The military ratchet was the most important single influence in raising prices and reducing the value of money in the past 1,000 years, and for most of that time debasement was the most common, but not the only, way of strengthening the 'sinews of war'." (page 646)

However, despite its importance, military expenditure has not been the only cause of inflation, nor has it been the most important in every case.

One of the author's main themes is the problem of simultaneously trying to control the quality and quantity of money. He discusses many cases of inflation over the past couple of thousand years and identifies several (not necessarily mutually exclusive) causes. These are:

- Conflict between the Interests of Debtors and Creditors.
- The Fungibility of Money
- The Population Explosion
- The Military Ratchet
- The Developmental Money Ratchet

As a result of the above-mentioned factors the supply of money tends to alternate in every age between too little and too much, with the pendulum swinging from excessive concern with the quality of money to the opposite extreme of an inflationary, excessive quantity of money.

This is the basis of the author's Pendulum Meta-Theory of money, i.e. a "general theory comprising sets of more limited, partial theories, which spring out of the special circumstances of their time.

The enveloping pendulum or metatheory also explains why the usual theories of money, despite being so confidently held at one time, tend to change so drastically and diametrically (and therefore so puzzlingly to the uninitiated) to an equally accepted but opposite theory within the time span appropriate to historical investigation."

7

BANKING SECTOR AND FINANCIAL SYSTEM

INTRODUCTION

Only recently have researchers started to address the general questions of the optimal design of the financial system and the optimal scope of financial intermediaries. The predominant role that banks have long played in financial intermediation led researchers to focus for many years on the development of theories explaining the existence of these intermediaries. This in turn has shaped the research both on the motives for regulating banks and on the role of capital regulation.

DESIGN OF THE FINANCIAL SYSTEM

Economic theory has traditionally focused on the real sector of the economy and disregarded the role of financial intermediation, viewing it as a veil. Effectively, in a world à la Arrow-Debreu, where markets are complete, information is symmetric and other frictions are not present, there is no room for financial intermediaries. However, the world we live in is quite different from that envisioned by Arrow and Debreu, which explains the increasing evidence of financial intermediaries' influence in the economy. This evidence has manifested itself in various different ways, ranging from a strong correlation between the size of the financial system and the level of the country's economic development (King and

Levine (1993)) to differences in the way firms finance investment in bank-based systems (systems where banks predominate) and market-based systems (those where financial markets predominate) (Mayer (1988)).

Despite the interest in the configuration of the financial system that such evidence has generated, our understanding of the interlinkages between the various parts of that system remains limited because research on the optimal design of the financial system is still in its early stages and has been hampered by the complexity of the problems involved.2 Nevertheless, researchers have already made significant progress explaining, for example, the parallel existence of financial intermediaries and markets, the differences between bank-based systems and market-based systems and the role of various financial intermediaries.

As for the research on financial intermediaries, it focused initially on the development of theories to explain commercial banks but has more recently been extended its goals to a study of the implications of broadening the scope of these intermediaries to include activities such as investment banking, insurance and commerce. Notwithstanding all this progress, the research on bank capital regulation continues to focus on intermediaries that combine lending with deposit taking.

The Existence of Banks

In a world à la Arrow-Debreu with complete and frictionless markets, there would be no need for financial intermediaries because investors and borrowers would be able to achieve efficient risk allocation on their own. It is necessary to modify the assumptions underlying this framework and assume the presence of some frictions in order to justify the existence of financial intermediaries. In the earlier theories of banks, these frictions result from transaction costs. In the contemporary theories, they arise instead from informational asymmetries.

In earlier theories of financial intermediation, such as Gurley and Shaw's (1960), the main activity of intermediaries would be the transformation of securities issued by firms (shares and bonds) into securities demanded by investors (deposits). Financial intermediaries are valuable because they provide services of divisibility and risk transformation, which borrowers cannot obtain on their own under identical conditions due to transaction costs. For example, if there are fixed costs associated with any financial transaction, borrowers will form coalitions to sell together in order to save on these costs. If there are indivisibilities in the transaction technology, a coalition of investors will be able to build a more diversified portfolio, that is, one with lower risk than the portfolio each member is able to build on its own.

In modern theories of financial intermediation, the two most prominent explanations for the existence of intermediaries like depository institutions are the provision of liquidity and the provision of monitoring services.6 Banks are valuable as providers of liquidity services because they provide depositors with liquidity insurance (Bryant (1980) and Diamond and Dybvig (1983)). By issuing demand deposits, banks can improve on a competitive market because these deposits allow for better risk-sharing among households that face idiosyncratic shocks to their consumption needs over time.

The importance of banks in this framework arises from an information asymmetry: the shock that affects a household's consumption needs is not publicly observable. Banks are valuable as providers of monitoring services because they act as delegated monitors to investors and thus avoid the duplication of monitoring costs, (Diamond (1984)). As with the liquidity insurance explanation, the key to the existence of banks in this setup is also an informational problem.

Firms are assumed to have more information about their investment projects than investors do.

Investors can learn this information but only after incurring a monitoring cost. They may choose, however, to delegate monitoring to a bank, through which they all provide funding to the firm. By acting as delegated monitors of investors, banks save on monitoring costs and make funding available to firms at a lower cost than direct lending. The provision of liquidity insurance explains the liability side of the bank's balance sheet and the provision of monitoring services explains the asset side of the balance sheet.

None of these approaches, however, puts forward an explanation as to why it is advantageous for an intermediary to offer both of these services, as happens with the existing depository institutions. Diamond and Rajan (1998) address this issue in a model where both investors and borrowers care about liquidity.

The former are concerned with liquidity because they are uncertain about the time at which they may want to reduce their holdings of a financial asset, while the latter are concerned with liquidity because they are uncertain about their ability to raise added funding in the future. An intermediary that accepts deposits and extends loans is valuable in that setting because it enables depositors to have better access to their funds than they would if they invested directly in firms, and it insures borrowers against the risk that funding will be cut off prematurely, which they would face had they borrowed from an investor.

In conclusion, the research on the design of the financial system reviewed in this section shows that financial institutions and markets are not perfect substitutes, thus confirming that the configuration of the financial system matters. Therefore, any change to one of these institutions, for example through regulations, is bound to have implications far beyond the institution itself.

Despite this, researchers continue to focus on financial intermediation through banks. This is motivated partly by the role of banks, which are still perceived to be the most important intermediaries, and partly for simplifying reasons because models rich enough to encompass various forms of intermediation become highly complicated very quickly.

Do Banks need to be Regulated?

The justification for any regulation usually stems from a market failure such as externalities, market power or asymmetry of information between buyers and sellers. In the case of banking, there is still no consensus on whether banks need to be regulated and, if so, how they should be regulated. This partly reflects the lack of consensus on the nature of the market failure that makes free banking not optimal. Nonetheless, there are two justifications that are often presented for regulating banks: the risk of a systemic crisis and the inability of depositors to monitor banks.

The Systemic Risk Argument

Banks' provision of liquidity services leaves them exposed to runs (Diamond and Dybvig (1983)). The reason is that a bank needs to operate with a balance sheet where the liquidation value of its assets is less than the value of liquid deposits in order to provide liquidity services. Under these circumstances, given that depositors' expectations about the value of their deposits depend on their place in line at the time of withdrawal because of the first come, first served rule, a run can occur without the release of adverse information about the bank's assets and even when there is perfect information about the bank's assets. For example, if depositors panic, they may try to withdraw their funds out of fear that other depositors will do so first, thus forcing an otherwise sound bank into bankruptcy. If there were no aggregate uncertainty and if each bank's investment in the short-term asset were publicly observable then depositors could be fully insured against the liquidity risk faced by their bank if banks could lend to each other (Bhattacharya and Gale (1987)).

However, when there is asymmetry of information about the banks' assets, as happens when banks provide monitoring services because this requires them to hold a large portion of their assets in the form of illiquid loans, the interbank market will not generally be able to provide depositors with full liquidity insurance.

A possible reason is that under these conditions, banks are afraid of a "winner's curse" (that is, of lending only to other banks that have already been rejected loans because of their poor quality) and consequently lend less than they would under homogeneous information (Flannery (1996)). Asymmetry of information about banks' assets makes them susceptible to an additional source of runs, the release of information on the value of those assets, (Jacklin and Bhattacharya (1988)). A bank run that is triggered by the release of information indicating poor performance by the bank may be beneficial because it is a source of discipline.

In contrast, a run triggered by depositors' panic or by the release of information when there is asymmetry of information among depositors about bank returns will not be beneficial. In this case, the run is costly because it forces the premature liquidation of assets, thus disrupting the production process. Furthermore, it may trigger contagion runs, which may culminate in a system failure. It is this risk of a system failure that forms the basis of the classical argument proposing mechanisms to insure banks against liquidity shocks despite their interference in the free functioning of markets.

Proposals to Insulate Banks from Runs

One of these proposals suggests the development of narrow banks, that is, banks that invest only in riskless securities, such as short-term government securities. Narrow banks are run-proof but this comes at a cost in that they do not perform one of banks' key functions, the creation of liquidity. Another drawback associated with narrow banking results from the inability of intermediaries to exploit the gains that result from combining deposit-taking with lending extended through commitments or credit lines (Kashyap, Rajan and Stein (1999)). Moreover, it is possible that the new firms that would move in to fill the vacuum left by banks would inherit the problem of runs (Diamond and Dybvig (1986) and Wallace (1996)).

Another proposal suggests funding banks with equity rather than demand deposits. This would make banks immune to runs but would be costly, as under certain conditions demand deposits dominate equity contracts in insuring consumers against random shocks to their intertemporal preferences for consumption

(Jacklin (1987)). This proposal, therefore, yields a trade-off between stability and efficiency.

A third proposal builds on the suspension of convertibility. If banks could precommit not to liquidate more than the portion of their assets that is necessary to meet the liquidity demands of those consumers that wish to consume early then they would eliminate the other consumers' incentive to run on the bank. Suspension of convertibility, though, provides complete insurance only if liquidity shocks are perfectly diversifiable and if the portion of consumers that wish to consume early is known. A fourth proposal, probably the oldest one, is associated with Bagehot (1873), who is usually credited with the first analysis of a central bank's role as lender of last resort (LLR) in preventing a bank run from turning into a panic.

To that end, he argues that the central bank should make clear in advance its readiness to lend any amount to a bank that is having liquidity problems provided the bank is solvent. Lending should be done at a penalty rate (to reduce banks' incentives to use these loans to fund normal business) and only against good collateral (valued at pre-panic prices).

It appears, however, that the conditions set out by Bagehot for operating the LLR function impede the LLR from attaining its key objective. A bank with good collateral will be able to borrow from the market. It is when there is some uncertainty about the bank's financial condition that the bank may not be able to meet its liquidity needs in the interbank market and therefore an LLR becomes valuable (Flannery (1996)). In Bagehot's own words: "Every Banker knows that if he has to prove that he is worthy of credit, however may be his argument, in fact his credit is gone" (p. 68). The LLR could avoid this problem by committing to extend liquidity support to all the banks seeking it, but this would come at a cost, as it would lead to moral hazard.

A final proposal to protect banks from runs is for the government to offer deposit insurance (Diamond and Dybvig (1983)).18 A government scheme of full insurance guarantees banks complete protection from runs. However, such a scheme is not socially costless because the government will have to tax other sectors of the economy, and therefore leads to a possible deadweight loss, when it is asked to provide liquidity as a result of a bank's low return or of large early withdrawals. Deposit insurance, in addition, may lead to moral hazard.

Deposit Insurance and Moral Hazard

Government deposit insurance has proven very successful in protecting banks from runs, but at a cost because it leads to moral hazard. By offering a guarantee that depositors are not subject to loss, the provider of deposit insurance bears the risk that they would otherwise have borne. As a result, it diminishes depositors' incentive to monitor banks and to demand an interest payment commensurate with the risk of the bank. Furthermore, when the insurance scheme charges the bank a flat rate premium, the bank does not internalise the full cost of risk and therefore it has an incentive to take on more risk.

Merton (1977) pioneered the use of the arbitrage pricing method, originally developed for pricing options on common stock, to analyse the deposit insurance distortion on banks' risk-taking incentives. He shows that deposit insurance can be viewed as a put option on the value of the bank's assets with a striking price equal to the promised maturity value of its debt.

If the insurance premium is risk-insensitive, the bank can increase the value of the put option by increasing the risk of its assets and/or decreasing its capital-to-assets ratio. A bank's appetite for risk is further increased with an increase in competition in the banking sector and a reduction in the value of the bank's charter (Marcus (1984) and Keeley (1990), Hellmann, Murdock and Stiglitz (1997), and Matutes and Vives (1998)).

The trade-off introduced by deposit insurance - ruling out bank runs at the expense of moral hazard - has motivated proposals to change the design of the deposit insurance scheme or introduce complementary regulations aimed at reducing the moral hazard while maintaining the protection to depositors.

The most frequent proposals to deal with the moral hazard caused by deposit insurance are to charge banks risk-related insurance premiums and to regulate their capital structure.

Is Fairly Priced Deposit Insurance Possible?

To eliminate the risk-shifting incentive it gives banks, deposit insurance needs to be fairly priced. However, as we are about to see, asymmetry of information may make the computation of fair premiums impossible or undesirable from a welfare point of view.

Starting with Merton (1977), a vast literature has used the arbitrage pricing method to determine the fair insurance premium. The arbitrage pricing method assumes that, among other things, the financial markets are complete, the provider of deposit insurance has perfect information about the risk of banks' assets, it can value accurately banks' assets, and moral hazard is explicitly or implicitly ruled out. Under these conditions, however, deposit insurance is not necessary because there is no risk of bank panics.

For that reason researchers began to study the feasibility of fairly priced deposit insurance where there is asymmetry of information. Chan, Greenbaum and Thakor (1992), for example, consider a setting where there is asymmetry of information and the insurance provider offers a menu of contracts, each requiring the bank to hold a certain capital-to-assets ratio and charging it a given insurance premium per unit of deposits it holds. The authors find that it is generally impossible to implement incentive-compatible, fairly priced deposit insurance in that setting. When there is only adverse selection, the impossibility arises because banks are indifferent vis-à-vis their capital structure when insurance is fairly priced. Therefore, they prefer a lower insurance premium for any positive level of deposits. Because of this, the high-risk institution always prefers the menu of contracts chosen by the low-risk institution as long as this one chooses some positive level of deposits.

Freixas and Rochet (1995) consider the issue of incentive-compatible fair pricing of deposit insurance in a more general framework, where banks are valuable because they manage deposits. They show that fair pricing is feasible but is not desirable from a welfare point of view. The reason is that it entails a subsidisation of the less efficient banks by the more efficient ones. This cross-subsidisation prevents the less efficient banks from mimicking the more efficient ones, thus improving the allocation of deposits, but it is distortionary because it leads to inefficient entry and exit decisions.

The Depositors' Representative Argument

The systemic risk argument builds on the instability that arises with banks' provision of monitoring and liquidity services, which leaves them with a balance sheet that combines a large portion of liabilities in the form of demand deposits with a large portion of assets in the form of illiquid loans. Dewatripont and Tirole (1993a, 1993b) propose a rationale for banking regulation - the representation hypothesis - that builds instead on the corporate governance problems created by the separation of ownership from management and on the inability of depositors to monitor banks. The departing point of their argument is that banks, like most businesses, are subject to moral hazard and adverse selection problems. Therefore, it is important that investors monitor them. Monitoring, however, is expensive and requires, among other things, access to information.

Furthermore, it is wasteful when duplicated by several parties. In the case of banking, this is complicated by the fact that bank debt is mainly held by unsophisticated depositors without the necessary information to perform efficient monitoring. In addition, because most of them hold only a small deposit they have little incentive to perform any of the functions that monitoring a bank would require. This free-riding problem creates a need for a private or public representative of depositors. That need can be met by a regulation that mimics the control and monitoring that depositors would exert if they had the appropriate information, were sophisticated and fully coordinated.

In sum, the research reviewed in this section shows that banks provide superior intertemporal risksharing when they fund themselves with demand deposits. Under these conditions, however, bank runs and panics may develop as an equilibrium phenomenon. Because these are costly, several mechanisms have been proposed to rule them out. These mechanisms, however, are themselves costly.

For example, government deposit insurance can provide depositors full insurance but is a source of moral hazard. These problems are usually presented as one of the reasons for regulating banks. Another common rationale for banking regulation builds on the problems that the separation of ownership from management raises for corporate governance. In the case of banks, these problems are compounded by the fact that depositors are not in a position to monitor management, as they are small and uninformed.

Therefore, they need to be represented by a regulator.

The Regulation of Bank Capital

Since Modigliani and Miller's seminal contribution in 1958 showing that in a frictionless world with full information and complete markets the value of a firm is independent from its capital structure, researchers have studied the implications of deviations from that world for a firm's optimal capital structure. Taxes, costs of financial distress, imperfections in the product markets, transactions costs and asymmetry of information problems are just some examples of the frictions that researchers have considered to explain a firm's capital structure. In the case of banks, they have also considered two other factors: banks' access to the safety net, in particular to deposit insurance, and the fact that small, generally uninformed investors hold most of the bank debt.

Capital Regulation and the Systemic Risk Argument

As we have seen, deposit insurance, when not fairly priced, gives banks an incentive to increase risk, which they can accomplish, for example, by increasing the risk of their assets or their leverage. This risk-shifting incentive, together with the potential externalities resulting from bank failures, has been one of the main justifications for regulating bank capital.

The earlier literature on bank capital regulation, such as Kahane (1977), Kareken and Wallace (1978) and Sharpe (1978), studies the effectiveness of capital standards in controlling banks' solvency in complete market, state preference models. This literature creates a role for capital regulation by introducing deposit insurance. Depositors are fully insured and, therefore, have no incentive to adjust the demanded returns for the risk undertaken by the bank.

Because the insurance provider charges banks a flat insurance premium it gives them an incentive to increase risk. A problem with this rationale for capital regulation is that when markets are complete and there is no information asymmetry the need for deposit insurance is unclear and when it exists it can be appropriately priced, which eliminates the risk-shifting incentive.

This led researchers to start studying capital regulation in incomplete market settings. Some researchers adopted the portfolio approach of Pyle (1971) and Hart and Jaffee (1974), which models the bank as a portfolio of securities.

Bankers choose the composition of their portfolios in order to maximise the expected profit for a given level of risk, taking the yields of all securities as given. Koehn and Santomero (1980) and Kim and Santomero (1988) adopt this approach and assume, as a proxy for the incompleteness of markets, that bankers are risk-averse and therefore maximise a utility function of the bank's financial net wealth.

A possible justification for this proxy is that the bank is owned and managed by the same agent, which cannot completely diversify the risk. The introduction of a flat capital requirement restricts the risk-return frontier of the bank, forcing it to reduce leverage and to reconfigure the composition of its portfolio of risky assets.

This may lead to an increase in the bank's probability of failure because the banker may choose to compensate the loss in utility from the reduction in leverage with the choice of a riskier portfolio. Regulators can eliminate this adverse effect by requiring banks to meet a risk-based capital requirement instead. The conclusion by this literature that more stringent capital standards could lead to an increase in the bank's risk of failure drew a great deal of attention, but it was subsequently questioned on several grounds. Rochet (1992) questions two features of the Pyle-Hart-Jaffee model adopted in this literature. Bank capital is treated in the same way as any other security, implying that banks can buy and sell their own stock at a given price, regardless of their investment policy, and banks choose their policies as if they were fully liable.

Rochet shows that when limited liability is taken into account and bank capital is exogenously set at a certain level, the convexity of preferences due to limited liability may dominate risk aversion, and the bank, if undercapitalised, will behave as a risk lover.

In this case, even a risk-based capital regulation that makes use of "market-based" risk weights (that is, weights proportional to the systematic risks of the assets as measured by their market betas) may not be enough to restrain the bank's appetite for risk.28 It may be necessary to impose an additional regulation, for example, to require banks to operate with a minimum capital level. Furlong and Keeley (1989) and Keeley and Furlong (1990) also question the adverse effect of more stringent capital standards, arguing that this result does not hold when the possibility of bank failure and the effects of changes in the value of the deposit insurance put option are appropriately considered.

The authors use a value-maximising model where a bank with publicly traded stock maximises the value of its stock. They show that the bank never increases portfolio risk as a result of increased capital standards when it pays a flat rate deposit insurance premium. The reason is that the marginal value of the deposit insurance option with respect to asset risk declines as leverage declines.

Therefore, an increase in capital standards reduces the bank's incentive to take risk. A key aspect of modern banking theory not considered in this literature is the existence of information asymmetries. These are important because they are directly related to the existence of banks. As we saw previously, an important function of banks is to screen and monitor loans. The returns of these loans then become private information to bank managers, giving them discretion in the choice of the screening and monitoring intensities of loans.

This discretion can lead to various forms of moral hazard when a bank management's incentives are distorted, as happens when there is deposit insurance. Gennotte and Pyle (1991) consider the role of asymmetry of information by assuming that it prevents some firms from accessing the capital markets. Banks, however, can monitor these firms and thus make positive NPV loans.

This contrasts with the previous literature, where banks invest in zero NPV assets (because these are traded on perfect capital markets). Banks finance themselves with insured deposits and thus have their incentives distorted towards risk-taking. An increase in capital standards now has an ambiguous effect on the probability of failure. The induced increase in the portfolio risk may be outweighed, depending on the relationship between the NPV of loans and bank's investment in loans, by the effect of the reduction in the bank size.

Santos (1999) also considers the role of information asymmetry, but in a model where there is a principal-agent problem between the bank and the borrowing firm. The optimal contract the bank uses to fund that firm involves a combination of a loan and an equity stake in the firm. This contract is distorted by the fact that the bank funds itself with insured deposits.

An increase in capital standards leads the bank to adjust this contract to account for the higher costs it will incur in case of bankruptcy (as it is forced to operate with lower leverage) and the higher cost of funding (as capital is more expensive than deposits). This adjustment in the financing contract induces the firm to lower its risk, which in turn reduces the bank's risk of insolvency.

The previous papers assume that banks are owned and managed by the same agent or that there are no conflicts of interest between management and shareholders. Besanko and Kanatas (1996) study the implications of this assumption. In their model, bank insiders own only a fraction of the bank equity and take unobservable actions that maximise their own welfare. In that setting, higher capital standards have the usual asset substitution effect, leading, for a given asset base, to a reduction in the risk of the bank's assets. They also have the additional effect of reducing the bank insiders' effort as their equity stake decreases with the bank's issuance of equity to meet the new standards.

This dilution effect has a negative impact on the bank's solvency, which in some cases outweighs the asset substitution effect. Information frictions can also give rise to adverse selection problems. Bensaid, Pagès and Rochet (1995) consider both the presence of an adverse selection problem, as the quality of the bank's assets is private information of the bank's owner, and a moral hazard problem, as the bank's profits depend on the unobservable effort chosen by the banker. In contrast with most of the previous literature that focuses on the solvency effects of capital regulation, their main goal is to find the efficient solvency regulation that minimises the dead-weight losses of running deposit insurance. They find that optimal regulation can be decentralised by offering banks a menu of solvency and quality requirements.

Solvency requirements need to be risk-adjusted and quality requirements are defined in terms of (soft) interim information, measured, for instance, by ratings performed by independent agencies.

The literature reviewed above uses a partial equilibrium analysis and therefore does not capture the costs to the other sectors of the economy of an increase in the demand for capital due to capital standards. Gorton and Winton (1995) show that these costs may lead the regulator to set a capital standard lower than that called for by stability considerations alone.31 Banks in their model provide liquidity by offering demand deposits and produce information about borrowers which is lost if they fail or leave the industry. In choosing the capital standards, the regulator faces two problems: one deriving from banks' participation incentives (negative externalities from bank failures make their social charter value higher than the private value, giving shareholders less incentive to raise capital than the regulator) and the other from the imperfect substitutability between capital and deposits. Increasing capital standards reduces the risk of failure (this is both privately and socially desirable because the bank's charter value is lost less often), but it reduces deposits (this is costly because these securities are less informationally sensitive than bank capital and therefore they economise on the "lemons cost" that agents incur when trading in the latter).

From the 1988 Accord to the Basel Committee's 1999 Proposal for a New Framework

The 1988 Basel Capital Accord has made an important contribution to the prominence of bank capital regulation. The Accord has been praised, for example, for promoting the international convergence of capital standards and for improving these standards in many countries. Over time, however, its conceptual limitations together with financial innovation have created incentives and opportunities for regulatory capital arbitrage, and have consequently led to a reduction in its effectiveness. This has prompted a debate on the design of capital standards and put pressure on the regulatory authorities to revise the Accord. This debate focused initially on the alternative approaches to setting capital standards put forward in the literature, but since the mid-1999 it has centred on the Basel Committee's proposal for a new capital adequacy framework.

The 1988 Capital Accord and its Amendments

In the early 1980s, as concern about international banks' financial health mounted and complaints of unfair competition increased, the Basel Committee on Banking Supervision started considering proposals to set capital standards for these banks.36

An agreement was reached in July 1988, which was phased in by January 1993.

The 1988 Accord explicitly considered only credit risk. It required international banks from the G10 countries to hold a minimum total capital equal to 8% of risk-adjusted assets, with at least half of this met by tier 1 capital (equity capital and disclosed reserves).37 Tier 2 capital could include, among other instruments, hybrid debt capital instruments. Risk-adjusted assets were defined as the sum of the riskadjusted assets on and off balance sheet. On-balance sheet assets were assigned to one of four risk buckets (0%, 20%, 50% and 100%) and then weighted by the bucket's weight. Off-balance sheet contingent contracts, such as letters of credit, loan commitments and derivative instruments, which are traded over the counter, needed to be first converted to a credit equivalent and then multiplied by the appropriate risk weight.

Over time, the Accord has been fine-tuned to account for financial innovation and some of the risks it did not consider initially. For example, it was amended in 1996 to require banks to set aside capital to cover the risk of losses arising from movements in market prices. This amendment also defined a tier 3 capital to cover market risks, and allowed banks to count subordinated debt (with an original maturity of at least two years) in this tier.

The main novelty of this amendment relates to the fact that it allows banks to use, as an alternative to the standard approach, their internal models to determine the required capital charge for market risk. The standard approach defines the risk charges associated with each position and specifies how these charges are to be aggregated into an overall market risk capital charge. The internal models approach, in contrast, allows a bank to use its model to estimate the value-at-risk (VaR) in its trading account, that is, the maximum loss that the portfolio is likely to experience over a given holding period with a certain probability. The market risk capital requirement is then set based on the VaR estimate.

Alternative Approaches to Set Capital Standards

When the Accord was introduced in 1988, its design was questioned because, among other things, the capital ratios appeared to lack economic foundation, the risk weights did not reflect accurately the risk of the obligor and it did not account for any benefits from diversification. Over time, new concerns emerged about the Accord because financial innovation made it increasingly easier for banks to find "cosmetic" adjustments to boost their reported capital ratios without enhancing their soundness (Jones (2000)).

Growing evidence on these shortcomings, together with the experience accumulated since the Accord was introduced and the research undertake in the mean time, prompted the development of various alternative approaches to the Accord's "buckets" framework for setting capital standards, (Mingo (2000)). Under one of these approaches, the internal ratings-based approach (IRBA), banks would assign a rating to each borrower based on their rating models and estimate the probability of default (PD) for each of the ratings they define. Regulators would then define a function to convert this vector of PDs into the minimum required capital.

Another approach, the full models approach (FMA), would extend to credit risk (and possibly other risks) the Accord's approach for market risks. Banks would need to develop a system to estimate (either independently or jointly) the probability density functions for losses in all of the bank's business (housed in the banking and trading book) stemming from each of the risk categories. The regulator would then set the capital requirement so that a given soundness objective, for example a minimum solvency standard, is met.

Finally, some have suggested using the "pre-commitment" approach (PCA). This approach was initially designed as an alternative to the internal models approach for market risks (Kupiec and O'Brien (1995)). Under the PCA, a bank would pre-commit to a maximum loss exposure over a period of time and the capital charge would be defined as a function of that loss exposure. Should the bank incur a larger loss, it would be subject to a penalty, which could take the form of monetary fines, punitive capital charges or other restrictions on future trading activities.

How do these approaches compare with the 1988 Basle Accord? As we saw above, that Accord adopted a "buckets" approach, treating all banks alike, and thus not giving safer banks the incentive to distinguish themselves from riskier ones in order to save on capital. Moreover, the definition of buckets based on the asset category that it adopted, a criterion only loosely related to risk, further heightened banks' incentive to develop regulatory capital arbitrage practices. The IRBA represents an improvement over that approach because it defines the buckets based on a risk measure rather than on the asset's category.

As a result, it would bring regulatory capital requirements for each exposure into closer alignment with the risk of the underlying asset and would give banks better incentives to improve on their risk management practices, as this would be reflected in capital savings. However, the extent of this advantage depends partly on the way regulators map the information produced by banks' internal models into the regulatory capital. For example, if they were to set capital requirements only for a reduced number of rating buckets, this would reduce, but not eliminate, incentives for regulatory capital arbitrage.46 An additional shortcoming of the IRBA is, as with the framework in the 1988 Accord, its inability to account for differences across institutions in such things as the portfolio's diversification.

The FMA and the PCA do not suffer from these problems, but they have their own drawbacks.

Though conceptually different, the two approaches are related (Rochet (1999)). In the FMA, the back testing validation procedure (including the penalties in case the bank fails the test) needs to give the bank the incentive to reveal truthfully the probability density function of its portfolio's losses, which the regulator would then use to set the capital requirement. In the PCA, the penalty function needs to give the bank the incentive to choose the capital requirement that the regulator would have imposed had it known the density function of the bank's portfolio of losses. A challenge to both approaches is that to be incentive-compatible the back testing procedure and the penalty function have to be bank- specific, which raises questions of feasibility.

The FMA is more intrusive in management and requires banks to release more information. The PCA in contrast, because it applies penalties ex post, is more prone to a time consistency problem. Regulators, for example, would be pressured to waive the penalty in case it were to lead to bankruptcy. In addition, because of limited liability the approach does not protect against go-for-broke strategies.

In sum, the new approaches to setting capital standards move away from the "one-size-fits-all" approach of the original Basel's Capital Accord. They all attempt to take account of the fact that banks are better informed about their risks than regulators. Some of them go even further and aim at designing incentive-compatible standards.

These approaches, however, in contrast with the literature on optimal regulation, do not consider other regulatory instruments. That literature suggests that the inclusion in the regulatory menu of instruments, such as deposit insurance, access to the lender of last resort, (soft) information (measured for instance by agencies' ratings) and possibly the set of services banks want to offer, would facilitate the design of a regulation giving banks the incentive to truthfully reveal their risk. Besides the conceptual differences between the various approaches, their implementation also raises different challenges regarding the modelling and measurement of credit risk as well as the data necessary to validate them. Despite giving consideration to the full models approach, these feasibility issues led the Basel Committee to opt for an approach based on banks' internal rating models in its proposal to revise the Accord.

The Basel Committee's Proposal to Revise the 1988 Accord

In June 1999, the Basle Committee released for comment its proposal for a new capital adequacy framework. The proposal consists of three pillars: minimum capital standards, a supervisory review process and effective use of market discipline (Basel Committee (1999c)).

The last pillar is intended to encourage banks to disclose information in order to enhance the role of market participants in monitoring banks. To that end, the Committee is proposing that banks disclose information on, among other things, their components of regulatory capital, risk exposures and risk-based capital ratios computed in accordance with the Accord's methodology.

The second pillar, the supervisory review process, is intended to ensure that a bank's capital position is consistent with its overall risk profile and to enable early intervention. According to the Committee, the review process should rest on a set principles, including the principle that supervisors expect banks to operate with capital above the regulatory minimum and should be able to require them to hold capital in excess of that minimum, and the principle that supervisors should seek to intervene at an early stage to prevent capital from falling below prudent levels.

The first pillar, the new capital requirements, aims at making capital charges more correlated with the credit risk of the bank's assets. The Committee also propose to develop capital charges for risks not considered in the current Accord, such as interest rate risk in the banking book and operational risk. Regarding credit risk, the Committee propose a new standardised approach and it has announced that it will propose an alternative approach based on banks' internal ratings frameworks.

The new standardised approach retains some parts of the 1988 Accord, such as the definitions of regulatory capital. Its major novelty is the replacement of the existing risk weighting scheme by a system where the risk weights are determined by the rating of the borrower, as defined for example by a rating agency. According to the proposed system, for each given class of borrowers, those with high ratings have a risk weight smaller than 100% but those with the lowest rating have a risk weight larger than 100%.

With respect to the Committee's proposal to set capital standards based on banks' internal ratings frameworks, its release is expected only in early 2001. However, the Committee has already announced that banks will have to meet a set of conditions in order to be considered for this approach and that the proposal will encompass at least two variants, a foundation and an advanced approach, with the latter relying on more parameters estimated by the banks' models.

It is outside the scope of this paper to provide a detailed analysis of the Committee's proposal, as this would require a full presentation of it. Moreover, some parts of it, particularly the standardized approach, have already been the subject of extensive analysis elsewhere. However, a comparison with the literature reviewed above shows that some of its insights seem to have been incorporated in the proposal, but others not. For example, the literature on the optimal regulation in settings where there is asymmetry of information shows that incentive compatibility calls for a menu approach instead of a "one-size-fits-all" rule.

The Committee's proposal appears to indicate a move in that direction. In addition to the standardised approach, it also includes the information that there will be an IRBA, which is a way of recognising that banks are better informed about their risks than regulators and of making use of that informational advantage. Furthermore, its decision to offer multiple variants of the IRBA meets one of the necessary conditions for offering banks a menu of regulations and the opportunity for them to distinguish themselves from their peers depending on their preferences.

Whether that menu will give banks the right incentives to reveal their true preferences rather than mimic other banks will depend, among other things, on the authorities' objective for offering multiple variants, their design, and the access and exit conditions.54 In this respect, the Committee's proposal, because it considers only capital adequacy, appears not to have taken into account the insight of the literature that in general it is advantageous to consider instruments other than capital standards in the menu. The inclusion of some of the instruments suggested in the literature, such as deposit insurance and access to the lender of last resort, however, goes beyond what supervisors themselves can do and would require the involvement of other authorities.

There are areas where the Committee's proposal could be in agreement with the literature, but some of the details that are still missing make this evaluation difficult. A case in point is the second pillar, the supervisory review process. One of its stated goals is "to enable early supervisory intervention if capital does not provide a sufficient buffer against risk". This idea of early intervention seems to resemble the insight of the literature on the role that capital standards can play in the optimal governance of banks. They can be used to define the trigger point for interference in management and transfer of control from shareholders to the depositors' representative, the supervisory authority.

According to the literature, however, both the trigger point and the forms of interference need to be specified ex ante. The Committee's proposal does not include similar definitions. In addition, the associated discretion can also be a source of problems in the principal-agent relationship between banks and supervisors.

Finally, there are those areas where it is still not possible to evaluate the new capital standards because the proposal is silent about them. That is the case of the minimum capital requirement. While the proposal states that the definition of capital will not be subject to changes, it does not state the criteria that will determine the minimum capital requirement and the corresponding objective.

REMARKS

Despite the progress in the research on banking since 1988, the year of the Basel Capital Accord, there is still no consensus on the optimal design of bank capital regulation. There are differences in opinion regarding the market failure that justify banking regulation. There are differences in the conclusions of the research on the optimal design of capital regulation, albeit explained by different modeling assumptions. In addition, there are still many relevant questions that remain unanswered. For example, we still lack a full understanding of the relative efficiencies of the various financial intermediaries in processing and aggregating information, and we also lack a complete understanding of the optimal risk-sharing among the various claimholders in a general equilibrium framework.

Notwithstanding these shortcomings, the research already undertaken, particularly that which builds on contemporary banking theory, has produced some useful insights for the design of capital standards. For example, it shows that raising the minimum required capital standards may improve banks' stability but it is a potential source of costs, some of which are rather subtle. Increasing the costs of operating in the banking business may lead to inefficiencies, as intermediation through other financial intermediaries is not a perfect substitute for that through banks. In addition, raising the share of bank capital in the economy may be costly, as securities are not perfect substitutes. The research also shows that there is value in considering banks' informational advantage. In this case, incentive compatibility calls for a regulation that encompasses a menu of different regulatory instruments.

Accordingly, in general, it will be advantageous to include in the menu instruments other than capital standards. Finally, a strand of that research points to the importance of capital standards in the implementation of the optimal governance of banks, as they can define the threshold for interference in management and for transfer of control from shareholders to the depositors' representative, the supervisory authority.

An analysis of the Basel Committee's proposal for a new capital adequacy framework reveals that some of these insights have made their way into the proposal, at least in a simplified form. This is evidenced in the replacement of the "one-size-fits-all" approach of the 1988 Accord with a more menu-like approach, offering banks different variants of the regulation. In contrast with the literature, however, the proposal's "menu" does not consider regulatory instruments other than capital standards. However, it is worth noting that in the case of some of the instruments suggested in the literature, such as those related to deposit insurance and the lender of last resort facility, their inclusion in the menu is beyond what supervisors can do on their own. Further evidence in the proposal of an insight of the literature is pillar two, the supervisory review process, which was introduced to enable early supervisory intervention. Here too, though, the proposal does not completely follow the literature, as it does not pre-specify both the trigger points and the corresponding forms of supervisory interference.

Finally, in a few areas, such as the minimum capital requirement, it is still not possible to evaluate the new regulation because the Committee's proposal is silent about them.

CAPITAL REGULATION IN CONTEMPORARY BANKING THEORY

The theoretical literature on bank capital regulation and analyses some of the approaches to redesigning the 1988 Basle Accord on capital standards. The paper starts with a review of the literature on the design of the financial system and the existence of banks. It proceeds with a presentation of the market failures that justify banking regulation and an analysis of the mechanisms that have been suggested to deal with these failures. The paper then reviews the theoretical literature on bank capital regulation. This is followed by a brief history of capital regulation since the 1988 Basle Capital Accord and a presentation of both the alternative approaches that have been put forward on setting capital standards and the Basel Committee's proposal for a new capital adequacy framework.

Banking is undoubtedly one of the most regulated industries in the world, and the rules on bank capital are one of the most prominent aspects of such regulation. This prominence results from the central role that banks play in financial intermediation, the importance of bank capital for bank soundness and the efforts of the international community to adopt common bank capital standards. Banks have always been the most important financial intermediaries in virtually all economies. This results from their role as providers of liquidity insurance and monitoring services and as producers of information. With respect to the regulation of bank capital, its importance derives, among other things, from the role it plays in banks' soundness and risk-taking incentives, and from its role in the corporate governance of banks. It also has to do with the influence of capital on the competitiveness of banks.

This influence was in fact one of the key factors behind the international efforts to harmonise capital standards in the 1980s. The international convergence of bank capital regulation started with the 1988 Basle Accord on capital standards. The G10 countries signed the Accord, which was intended to apply only to internationally active banks. Its focus was the measurement of capital and the definition of capital standards for credit risk. Since then the Accord has been endorsed by many other countries, been applied to many other banks and been subject to some amendments. It was amended in 1996 to cover market risks arising from banks' open positions in foreign exchange, traded debt securities, traded equities, commodities and options. In 1999, the Basel Committee on Banking Supervision released for comment a proposal to amend the Accord's original framework for setting capital charges for credit risk. In it, the Committee also proposed to develop capital charges for risks not taken into account by the present Accord, such as interest rate risk in the banking book and operational risk.

Since its introduction, the Capital Accord has been acknowledged for its contribution to the widespread use of risk-based capital ratios both as measures of the strength of banks and as trigger devices for supervisors' intervention, as in the prompt corrective action schemes in place. The Accord has also been praised for the international convergence of capital standards and for the improvement of these standards in many countries. Its design, however, has been blamed for several distortions to the business of banking. Growing evidence both on these distortions and on a reduction in the Accord's effectiveness, together with a better understanding of its conceptual shortcomings, has led to proposals to redesign it.

Despite the debate that such proposals have generated and the recent progress in the research on banking, there is still no consensus on how best to design the regulation of bank capital. This partly reflects differences in opinion as to the objectives of that regulation and the diverging results that researchers have unveiled regarding the optimal design of capital standards. It is also a reflection of our limited understanding of the implications of that regulation in general equilibrium frameworks.

Notwithstanding these shortcomings, the research already undertaken has produced some important guidelines for the design of capital standards. This paper contributes to the ongoing debate on bank capital regulation by reviewing both the contemporary banking literature that is most relevant to that debate and the theoretical literature on bank capital regulation. The paper also presents a brief analysis of the proposals that have been put forward to replace the Accord's original framework for capital standards for credit risk. The paper does not review the empirical literature on bank capital standards. For a review of this literature see, for example, Jackson et al (1999) and the references contained therein.

The remainder of the paper is organised as follows. The next section reviews the literature on the design of the financial system and the existence of banks. Section 3 discusses the market failures that justify banking regulation and presents the various mechanisms that have been suggested to address these failures. Section 4 reviews the literature on bank capital regulation and on the relationship between this regulation and the design of the deposit insurance scheme. Section 5 presents the 1988 Capital Accord and its main amendments. This is followed by a presentation of the alternative approaches to the Accord's original framework for credit risk that have been put forward and a brief description of the new capital adequacy framework that the Basel Committee has proposed to replace the 1988 Accord. Section 6 concludes.

Deposit Insurance Premium and Capital Standards: are they Related?

In the absence of moral hazard, if the insurance provider has perfect information about the risk of banks' assets it can attain actuarial soundness equally well with either a risk-based insurance premium or risk-related capital standards (Sharpe (1978)). However, when the insurance provider is able to observe bank risks only with error, these alternative pricing mechanisms are no longer equivalent (Flannery (1991)). This suggests that when there are information frictions it is advantageous to consider jointly the design of deposit insurance and capital requirements.

Giammarino, Lewis and Sappington (1993) consider this issue in a model where the banker knows the quality of the portfolio of loans but the regulator does not, and the banker can influence that quality through an unobservable effort choice. The objective of the regulator is to provide deposit insurance while maximising social welfare. In this case, it is valuable to determine jointly the insurance premium and capital standards. Under the socially optimal deposit insurance system, the insurance premium needs to be adjusted for the quality of the bank's portfolio of loans, and higher-quality banks are allowed a relatively larger asset base and face lower capital requirements. Freixas and Gabillon (1998) study the interplay between capital standards and deposit insurance when there is adverse selection and show that under the optimal regulation "low-quality" banks receive an implicit subsidy. They pay a high insurance premium but are not required to meet capital standards. "High-quality" banks, in contrast, have to meet minimum capital standards but pay a lower insurance premium.

The importance of having the insurance premium tied to capital standards in this setting stems from the fact that, because of the imperfect information, it pays to offer a regulation with a trade-off between the capital standards and the insurance premium in order to extract information and minimise the cost of inducing the low-quality banks to mimic the high-quality ones.

Bank Capital Regulation and the Depositors' Representative Argument

As explained above, Dewatripont and Tirole (1993a) justify the need to regulate banks because of the corporate governance problems arising from the separation of ownership from management. When frictions prevent the writing of complete contracts between shareholders and managers, the financial structure of a firm is important because it determines the allocation of control rights among the firm's claimholders. In the case of banks, an efficient allocation of control rights needs to take account of the fact that bank debtholders (depositors) are not in a position to monitor managers because they are small and uninformed. They need a representative.

In Dewatripont and Tirole's model, monitoring by the controlling party influences the manager's choice of effort, which is assumed to be unobservable. Effort is costly, but it improves the bank's performance. Bank managers do not care about monetary incentives, but they enjoy private benefits from running the bank in the absence of interference. The controlling party decides whether to interfere based on information it receives about the manager's effort.

Within this setup, the authors show that the optimal monitoring scheme threatens the manager with interference in the event of poor performance and guarantees him no interference as a reward for good performance. This can be implemented by leaving control with relatively passive claimholders (shareholders) when the bank performs well and transferring it to the more interventionist claimholders (the depositors' representative) in the event of poor performance.35

Key to this result is the fact that shareholders favour no interference (because their payoff is a convex function of profits), while depositors are more conservative (because their payoff is a concave function of profits).

Moreover, the lower the bank's solvency, the stronger the shareholders' bias towards risk and the weaker the depositors' bias against risk (depositors become almost like equityholders when the bank is very undercapitalised). Efficient regulation in this setup requires an increase in interference when bank performance deteriorates and includes a credible mechanism to transfer control to the regulator when the bank's solvency is low. The minimum solvency requirement could be part of such regulation if it defines the threshold for the transfer of control to the regulator. To sum up this section, deposit insurance is efficient in protecting banks from runs, but it distorts their incentives towards risk. This problem is one of the justifications for bank capital regulation. Earlier literature on capital standards models banks as portfolio managers that invest in zero NPV securities and focuses on the question of whether these reduce banks' risk of insolvency.

It finds mixed results, which have been questioned on the grounds that this literature neglects the special features of banks and assumes no asymmetry of information between banks and regulators. The research that models banks as firms that perform valuable services shows that increasing capital standards generally leads to an asset substitution effect that improves banks' solvency. Meeting the higher standards, however, is costly, for example because of a dilution effect, in which case the improvement may be reversed. Research in more general equilibrium settings shows that even though an increase in capital standards may improve banks' stability, it may not be desirable as it reduces deposits. This is costly because these are less informationally sensitive and therefore save on the "lemons cost" that agents incur when they trade in bank capital.

The literature on the optimal design of regulation finds results that are somewhat dependent on the regulator's social welfare objective and the information frictions. Some of its important insights are that because of the asymmetry of information the isomorphism between a risk-based insurance premium and risk-based capital standards no longer holds, and therefore exclusive reliance on either mechanism alone is sub-optimal. In general, the optimal regulation encompasses a menu of the regulatory instruments, designed to extract information from banks and minimise the cost of "bribing" the lower quality banks to mimic the higher quality ones.

Finally, there is a strand of literature which explains the role of capital standards based on the corporate governance problems in banks arising from the separation of ownership from management. Because depositors are not in a position to monitor bank managers, they need to be represented by the regulator. Capital standards may be an important instrument to implement the optimal governance of banks because they can be used to define the threshold for the transfer of control from shareholders to the regulator.

BIBLIOGRAPHY

Ariel Buira: *Challenges to the World Bank and IMF: Developing Country Perspectives*, London, Anthem Press, 2003.

Bouman, F.J.A.: *Small, Short and Unsecured: Informal Rural Finance in India*, Delhi, Oxford University Press, 1989.

Cooley, Thomas F.: *Frontiers of Business Cycle Research*, Princeton University Press, 1995.

Downs, Anthony: *An Economic Theory of Democracy,* New York, Harper and Row, 1957.

Gerald, K.: *The Less Developed Countries in the International Economy*, Cambridge, Cambridge University Press, 1975.

Greer, Douglas F.: *Industrial Organization and Public Policy,* MacMillan Publishing Company, 1992.

Guhan, S.: *The World Bank's Lending in South Asia*, Washington, Brookings Institution, 1995.

Hoshii, Iwao: *A Financial History of the New Japan*, Kodansha International Ltd., Lokyo, 1972.

Jha, P.R.: *Agriculture and Economic Development*, New Delhi, Ashish, 1988.

Le Prestre, Philippe: *The World Bank and the Environmental Challenge*, London, Associated University Presses, 1989.

Michael Connolly, *The International Monetary System: Choices for the Future*, New York, Praeger, 1983.

Ottomar, H.: *Distribution of Stock of Money,* Effingham, London, 1892.

Peet, Richard, Born, Beate: *Unholy Trinity: The IMF, World Bank, and WTO*, New York, Zed Books, 2003.

Ranade, Sudhanshu: *Rural Banking Adrift*, Bombay, Jaico Publishing House, 1984.

Rao, M.G. and R.J. Chelliah: *Survey of Research in Indian Fiscal Federalism*, National Institute of Public Finance and Policy, New Delhi, 1991.

Savla, Sandeep: *Money Laundering and Financial Intermediaries*, The Hague and Boston, Kluwer Law International, 2001.

Seligman, E. R. A. : *Currency Inflation and Public Debts*, New York, 1922.

Vines, David and Christopher Gilbert: *The IMF and its Critics: Reform of the Global Financial Architecture*, Cambridge, Cambridge University Press, 2004.

INDEX

□□□

cyber.tech
6/8/09